With compliments:

Derek Forbes.

THE ENIGMA
OF
JOHN BINGLEY'S POEM
"THE FAIR QUAKERS"
(1713)

Blot Publishing
69 Ware Road, HERTFORD, Herts SG13 7ED

ISBN 1 900929 01 5

Two Quaker pamphlets by the same author:

"A Nineteenth-Century Quaker Childhood and Other Memories:
A Conversation with Ann Taylor" (1985)

"Four Decades of Minutes: Hertford Preparative Meeting, 1951-
1991" (1991)

Both published for Hertford Preparative Meeting and obtainable
from Blot Publishing.

Printed in England by
Don Miles, 96 Marmion Road, Southsea, Hampshire PO5 2BB

THE ENIGMA

OF

JOHN BINGLEY'S POEM
"THE FAIR QUAKERS"
(1713)

AND A CHALLENGE TO QUAKER HISTORIANS

by Derek Forbes

With a foreword by Lorna Paulin

Blot Publishing
1996

List of Contents

Foreword *by Lorna Paulin*

Research, particularly when it is undertaken for pleasure, into any aspect of human activity is liable to lead into intriguing byways and alleys, and here is a delightful example. The poem, *The Fair Quakers*, by John Bingley or whoever, is a fascinating curiosity of English literature and of writings about Quakers. It presents one main enigma — who were the nineteen girls, identified tantalisingly only by the initials of their surnames and all somewhat fulsomely praised? — but there are also several others to ponder: did John Bingley write it? Who was John Bingley, anyway? Was he a Quaker? Did these evidently beautiful girls all belong to one Quaker Meeting? How could a poem like this be written about Quakers of all people, who, to put it mildly, tend only to praise characteristics other than physical beauty? The very title, *The Fair Quakers*, is almost a contradiction in terms.

It is not a great poem, but it is carefully written, with proper respect for heroic couplets, and an occasional gracefully rhythmic alexandrine. It uses eighteenth century poetic diction with some skill, avoiding merely stringing clichés together. If it had not been written in the shadow of the great, at the time of several celebrated writers and when Pope was producing some of his finest work, *The Fair Quakers* might well have been rated more highly. The possibility that no less a writer than Richard Steele is the "R. S." who agreed to write the verse foreword to the first edition of tile poem in 1713 seems to support this suggestion.

Derek Forbes has obviously much enjoyed finding this poem and considering the queries it raises, and his enjoyment is conveyed to the reader in a thoughtful and enlightening study.

vii

He examines the poem and the circumstances of its publication with punctilious care, but with a lightness of touch that shows what fun the whole project is. He faces all the enigmas involved, and he is brave enough even to consider that *The Fair Quakers*, to which he has devoted all this labour of love, might be a spoof, and a satire on Friends, though (rightly in my opinion) he does dismiss the idea. Derek Forbes realises, too, that associating the poem with Quakerism might have been intended to increase the sale of the publication, as Friends at the time were often the subject of curiosity and interest, as being different from other people in a strange yet worldly kind of way. There may be a parallel here with the Quaker Oats of our own time; the firm does not appear to have had any Quaker connections, but the name was presumably chosen to give an impression of healthy and cheerful living. This is borne out by the smiling elderly man in Quaker dress depicted on the packet, whose obvious excellent health is no doubt the result of consuming the contents.

The Fair Quakers described in the poem were evidently a delightful crowd, although they are described in such general terms that it is difficult to distinguish one from the other. One or two are praised for wit and eloquence as well as beauty, but the main impression given is that they were all charming and lovely. It may well be that their quakerliness, in appearance and behaviour, was a main cause of the poet's (and then the public's) interest in them.

Unusually, if not uniquely, the Society of Friends regarded men and women members as being on an entirely equal basis, right from its beginning. The responsible work as well as the menial tasks involved were shared by all, regardless of sex. This meant that women could use their intellectual as well as their domestic and practical gifts to the full, without being derided as "bluestockings", and were appreciated accordingly. There is no hint of this in *The Fair Quakers*, which is undeniably superficial and is not intended to be otherwise. It seems that John Bingley was not in sympathy with some of the principles and practices of the Society of which he was a member — if he was a Quaker at all. Plainness and simplicity were part of Quakers' way of life, being regarded as an aspect of their testimony of truth and certainly applicable to clothes. Indeed, some early Friends thought grey to be the only acceptable colour to wear, but

Margaret Fell spoke out, as early as 1700, against having to be "all in one dress and one colour: this is a silly poor Gospel". If Friends could afford it, their dresses, hats and bonnets were made of the finest materials, which must have helped even if the colours were dull. Dress, particularly of women Friends it seems, was a frequent subject for detailed discussion at business meetings and other gatherings. The pursuit of fashion was firmly discouraged, so much so that, for example, when neat small white aprons became fashionable in the eighteenth century Friends decided not to wear them, although until then they had been a usual part of their everyday dress.

A pretty girl's looks would be enhanced (as she was no doubt aware) by wearing plain, simple clothes, especially in contrast with the elaborate fashions of the time. A Quaker girl's appearance, and no doubt her reputation as well, would lead to her being regarded as both virtuous and unattainable, adding to the fascination and attraction. This was perhaps akin to the undying interest in nuns, still noticeable in our own contemporary scene — in their way of life, their simple dress, and their customs — even if there is no apparent desire to emulate them.

This study valuably includes not only the text of *The Fair Quakers* and the bitter and regrettable *Funeral Elegy* that appeared in the second edition, but also the whole of Josiah Martin's *Remarks on a Poem intituled The Fair Quakers* that followed the first edition in a matter of months. These *Remarks*, mainly in the form of a dialogue between Hilary, who rather likes the poem and Theophilus, who most certainly does not, take the work very seriously indeed. Theophilus regards it as "a very Licentious and heathenish Poem" and is "griev'd to consider the evil Consequence of it", and he brings Hilary round to his point of view, rather too easily I feel. If Theophilus was really expressing what most Friends would think about the poem at the time, they were sadly humourless. He was worried lest the girls depicted be led to Pride. It would be hard to prove that such a dire state of affairs resulted from the publication. It seems more likely that any Quaker girl, whose upbringing would encourage her to have a mind of her own, could size up a young man's compliments fairly accurately, and would allow for his being economical with the truth, rather in the way that a present-day girl receives a Valentine's Day message.

Derek Forbes helpfully sets the publication of the poem in the context of publishing and bookselling in the early eighteenth century, when poetry was widely read, and written too, by educated people of all ages. The reader's interest is maintained throughout the study by the writer's scholarship and wit. He has accomplished his task with meticulous care, but he does not overrate the importance of its subject. He admits that it has allowed him to devote little attention to the "lesser mundane events at this time" such as the death of Queen Anne, the Jacobite Rebellion of 1715.... It is refreshing to find literature given precedence for once over solemn affairs of state. Few studies throw such an intriguing challenge to the reader as this one, with the enigma(s) to be solved, as set out in the Introduction. Much ingenuity and investigation will be called for, but what a triumph it will be if answers are found!

Lorna Paulin

Introduction

Short extracts from *The Fair Quakers* were provided for Mollie Grubb to include in her anthology *Quakers Observed in Prose and Verse* (William Sessions Ltd., York, 1993). Otherwise, this unusual poem of 1713 seems to have been neglected, so far as present knowledge goes. As a piece in the classical mode, popular at the time, it is not discreditable, indeed it has charm; but it is not a great work of art. Its appeal to us today lies in its historical rather than its literary interest, and in the challenge of its enigma. This exploration of the poem and related circumstances is offered as much for the enjoyment of the general reader as for the stimulus of historical enthusiasts.

The author, supposedly John Bingley, provides conventional word-pictures of nineteen admired Quaker girls. The final one is the object of his particular adoration, though he fears that he may not be able to win her heart. After the poem's publication, Friends reacted against what was, to them at the time, its "licentiousness", though the piece is far from impure and the girls are left in shadow. A tract objecting to the poem was published by a known Friend, Josiah Martin, in 1714. Intended at that time to correct the harm the poem was thought to do, today the tract is especially valuable for revealing the attitudes to literature of a cultured and humane Quaker early in the eighteenth century. In 1715 a second edition of the poem appeared, with an extra piece that purported to be an elegy on Bingley's death from a broken heart following rejection by his favourite Fair Quaker.

A likely connection with Richard Steele is one of the poem's intriguing aspects. Chiefly, though, its fascination lies in the clues to the girls' identities given by cryptic sets of initials. In this lies a challenge to Quaker historians. The puzzle is set out in the text below but left for others to resolve. This could form an engaging quest for those who know the period. Its objects are delightful young ladies worth spending time with, even if, in the end, they prove untraceable. But if they can be traced — what treasures to add to early Quaker history! The writer would be glad to be notified of any positive results that may be achieved, c/o his home meeting at Hertford Friends' Meeting House, Railway Street, Hertford SG14 1BA. Librarians at Friends' House and Woodbrook should also be informed for the file. Hertford Preparative Meeting, which enjoys its tenure of Friends' oldest purpose-built and continuously-used Meeting House (1670), has history at its heart and takes a generous interest in this paper and its challenge. It offers a book-token for the first satisfactory solution.

The study that follows gives relevant extracts from the three printed sources, examines their validity, analyses their possible motivations and their achievements, and discusses their Quaker and worldly contexts. A hypothetical scenario for a hypothetical John Bingley is hazarded. The initialised names and clues are tabulated in Appendix One for ease of research; a brief evaluation of Bingley's verse and model examples of the poetry of the time are offered in Appendix Two; and reprints in full of the three documents on which this paper is based follow in the later appendices. Footnotes are excluded: all necessary citations are briefly given in the text.

Acknowledgements

I am grateful to Mollie Grubb for her initial interest in this topic, and to Hertford P.M. for being prepared to support the "challenge" with a book-token. Benefits to this paper, greatly appreciated, have come from the advice of my wife Adrienne, and from Violet Rowe, Neil Atkins, and Lorna Paulin, to the last of whom I am especially beholden for her kindness in writing the Foreword. I am obliged for their help to staff at Friends' House Library, especially Tabitha Driver, and as always to the staff and resources of the British Library. To my daughter Léonie Forbes, of Blot Publishing, I am indebted for her professional skill and care.

Chapter One

An introduction to the poem and
a consideration of its possible origins.

The Fair Quakers: A Poem is a surprising effusion of the early eighteenth century. It appears to have been written by a certain John Bingley. He is an otherwise unknown author who is described in the British Library catalogue as "writer of verses". The distinction is exact. The British Library does not rate Bingley a poet.

The first edition of this work is dated 1713. In 1714 Josiah Martin of Peel Meeting in London retorted with a Quaker tract, *Remarks On A Poem, Intitled, 'The Fair Quakers'* (hereafter shortened to *Remarks*). A second edition of *The Fair Quakers* appeared in 1715, augmented by a so-called *Funeral Elegy on the Death of John Bingley*. The author's name was given with the second edition, not the first. Short extracts from *The Fair Quakers* were contributed to Mollie Grubb's anthology, *Quakers Observed in Prose and Verse* (William Sessions Ltd., York, 1993). Apart from this, the poem and its attendant circumstances do not seem to have received attention. Yet they deserve it.

The Fair Quakers is, effectively, a love-poem in 376 lines. It celebrates the attractions of nineteen girls. Eighteen of them lead up to the poet's adored beauty who is the focus of the final 100 lines. All are supposedly young Friends. Abbreviated surnames give them some semblance of identity. (These are tabulated in Appendix One for ease of reference.) Do they have any historical reality, these girls — born in the lifetime of Margaret Fell, if not George Fox?

1

Bingley adopts the classical epic style from the beginning: "Aid, sacred Nymphs of the Pierian Spring!" He proceeds to a respectfully admiring glorification of the graces of each of the pseudo-anonymous Fair Quakers in a manner so glowing that we would call it outright Ovidian were it not for its sensual restraint. The effect is that of a court poem, scribed out by a conventionally-extravagant admirer sighing from a safe distance. Can this worldly piece really have the Quaker roots it claims?

An apparently integral link with Quakers is vouchsafed in the brief verse-foreword that forms part of the preamble. Apart from its title, the poem itself contains not a single clear reference to Quakerism. There is one ambiguity, the naming of "Victorious G--", which may or may not pertain to the most famous Quaker first-name initial. The *Remarks* tract, written by a Quaker, does not refute the poem's right to its title.

Sets of initials pose the most tantalising puzzle. The girls are referred to by what seem to be the first and last initials of their surnames, e.g. "O--d". A similar system is applied to certain other names. Three explicit sets of initials are given and can be easily identified, though they are not those of the Fair Quakers. They belong to three poets of past days, against whom Bingley recognises his deficiencies: "W--ll--r", Edmund Waller, royalist (*fl.* 1625-85), and two Elizabethans, "S--dn--y" and "G--v--lle", Sir Philip Sidney and Sir Fulke Greville. Why these three? Well, all three were famed for their mistress-smitten lyric sequences — Sidney for the "Astrophel and Stella" sonnets, Greville for his love poems in "Caelica", and Waller for his praises of, oh dear, his "Sacharissa". Bingley means to leave the reader in no doubt as to the poetic flights and indeed the poetic company to which, with due modesty, he aspires. Such modesty would certainly have been in order. Bingley's writing is not bad, but is pale in comparison with the work of real poets, as can be seen from the brief examples given in Appendix Two.

Before taking our consideration any further, it is best to sample the work itself, and note each of the initialised damsels in turn.

THE FAIR QUAKERS: A POEM

London: Printed for J. Morphew, near Stationers' Hall. MDCCXIII.

The Publisher to the Reader.

I am very well acquainted that the Excuses of a Friend's Importunity, or his stealing a Copy, or it having unadvisedly been distributed, and so committed privately to the Press, and the like, are so common and thread-bare, that they are grown a standing Jest: Yet, notwithstanding this, I will venture to assure the Readers of this following Poem, that this really is the Case, and that the Author of it will probably be later acquainted with the printing of it, and I am sure much more surprized than the Reader. For the truth is, I saw and was pleas'd with the Piece, which I found, in my Opinion, as well as in that of several much better Judges, to be Easy, Just, and entirely Novel. For which Reason I resolv'd without his Knowledge (whose Consent I was sure never to obtain) to thrust it into the Press: Which is the main Reason why you now find it made Publick. As for the Fate it may meet with in the World, the Author I am sure will be very little concern'd, nor I believe any one else, except the Bookseller and my self; He for his own Profit, and I, that (after this Presumption) I may look my Friend in the Face with better Assurance. So, Reader, I leave it with you, and wish you as much Pleasure in perusing it as I had.

- - - - - - - - - - -

Well, unknown Youth, hast thou thy Friends express'd,
And thy Fair Quakers like themselves hast dress'd:
Moving and soft, and gayly innocent;
Without Excess, yet full of Ornament.
Of youthful vertue thus proceed to write,
And by Example as by Verse invite.
With Innocence and Beauty grace your Strains,
The listening Isle shall bless your tuneful Pains:
Vertue resume her Sway and Vice retire,
And O--d reign, while thus she does inspire
The Friendly Muse, and guide the Quaker Lyre.

R.S.

3

These preambles present their own problems. It is not easy to decide how much weight to give to Morphew's disclaimer, which was a publishing cliché. And can "R.S." be Richard Steele? These matters will come under review later.

The Fair Quakers: A Poem

Aid sacred Nymphs of the Pierian Spring!	[line 1
While I no vulgar Theme attempt to sing....	
Conduct those Numbers, and direct those Lays	5
Which now I dedicate to Beauty's Praise.	
Thy kind Assistance too, soft God of Love,	
To me vouchsafe, thy Influence let me prove.	
Virgins from thee derive their various Charms,	
Their Eyes are thy bright Magazine of Arms....	
Instruct me then their Beauties to rehearse,	13
And let their Names immortalize my Verse....	
Fair O--d now too strongly does attest	19
Thy potent Sway, and wounds my suff'ring Breast:	
Thy Godhead I confess, oh! move the Fair	
To hear and be propitious to my Prayer;	
And thy bright Train, whilst I attempt to write,	
Assist my feeble Lays and guide my infant Flight.	

Begin, auspicious Muse, the pleasing Song,	25
Fir'd with new Beauties as thou go'st along.	
See lovely B--rs first in sight appears,	
A Blooming Virgin in her Prime of Years,	
Graceful her Shape, delightful is her Mien,	
An unaffected Smile, an Air serene	
Adorn her Face, where growing Charms are seen....	

"B--rs"? Bowers, Byers, *Bellers?* In 1713 the two unmarried daughters of John Bellers, according to George Clarke's recent book, namely Elizabeth and Theophila, were 23 and 18 respectively, and the poet is of course using "prime" in the sense of "springtime". That they may have possessed good looks is suggested by a portrait of Theophila. But few equations in Bingley's algebra of names are simple. We have to note that he writes of only one "B--rs". Elsewhere, with sisters, he mentions both, sometimes making their relationship clear, and sometimes leaving it to be inferred as with the two girls he mentions next.

Ma--n, with conqu'ring charms the Soul commands,   36
And captive leads the Heart in willing Bands....

Behold, a younger Ma--n comes in Sight,   48
Who shortly will shine forth with wond'rous Light;
Her budding Charms uncommon Lustre spread,
And beaming Glories crown her youthful Head....

Nor, W--n, shall thy Worth unsung remain,   55
Misfortunes never shall thy Lustre stain....
Each sundry Charm Adversity refines,   59
Like Diamonds set in Jet thy Vertue shines.

Young H--s appears, all innocently gay
Driving from ev'ry Breast Despair away....

P--n a fatal Splendour darts abroad....   71

Engaging M--re appears with artless Grace....   83

Next I advance to sing fair W--r's Name,   87
W--r whose Wit deserves immortal Fame....

Fair P--m next behold, serenely gay,   97
Pleasing as Summer's Shades and mild as May,
As Roses in their vernal Bloom appear,
To Sight and Smell delicious, sweet and fair,
Some with their Crimson Blush delight the View,
And others with their native Snowy Hue;
In P--m's Cheeks these Opposites unite,
The blushing Crimson and the snowy White....

— Hardly an original image, but nicely sustained. Little
wonder that a female Friend, the historian Dr Violet Rowe, with
whom this poem has been discussed, said, "I do think the girls
would like what he says about them!" So far, amorous young
Bingley is only half-way through his list of the vanguard. He
goes on to extol "T--r, the dazzling T--r" (l. 110) and "A younger
T--r" who shines "With a less fierce, but no less pleasing Light"
(l. 136). Even more so than the "fatal" P--n above, the elder
T--r is apparently a bit of a heart-breaker, proud and disdainful.
Scorned, her trembling lover emulates Orlando:

...Then to soft S--te Shades the Youth retires,   119
There, on the Barks of Trees, records his Fires:
And, Sorrow from his Bosom to remove,
Lov'd T--r's Name repeats in every Grove....

A bosky spot, S--te is the only place-name mentioned. Eight miles north of London lies Southgate, then a pleasantly-wooded area on the edge of Oakwood and Enfield Chase; but a gazetteer will throw up a dozen or more further possibilities all over the country. Our next invitation arrives:

See Ec--n all blooming, fair and young,   141
To whom unnumber'd budding Charms belong....

Here is the only three-syllabled name amongst those otherwise of one and two syllables, a circumstantial detail which supports a view that the author had the names of real people in mind. Eccleston? The praises continue:

...V--s whose Charms transcendent Joys diffuse....   150
But who shall sing her vast superiour Sense?   159
Her flowing Wit and pleasing Eloquence!...
Long may the Virgin, long with us remain,   166
With her soft Lyre to cure the poignant Pain,
And chear the Heart of every drooping Swain.

Young C--tt's Features Heav'nly Charms display,...
She wounds without Design each tender Breast,...   171
Yet tries no sly insinuating Arts   173
To gain a Conquest o'er unguarded Hearts....

O--n, the blooming O--n, comes in View,   191
One of the loveliest of the lovely Few....
Such radiant Charms bright ANNA did dispence,...   202

Anna, sister of O--n, is now dead, and receives her given name in full. She had been espoused by "youthful N--n, happy Man!" (l. 205). Anna blessed her sister before she died:

But the bright Charmer her Seraphick Mind   209
To Heaven, its native Seat, too soon resign'd:
Yet first her pious Thoughts she thus express'd,
    "On thee, Dear Sister, numerous Blessings rest,...
    One Kiss — farewel — I can no longer stay,   219
    My Guardian Angel summons me away:
    Heaven guide thee and protect thee —"
                                    There her Breath
Stop'd, and she smiling sunk into the Arms of Death.
The Powers above, propitious to her Prayer,
Have made fair O--n their peculiar Care....

Next comes one, "'Tis M--s, whose Beauty Love's great God disarms" (l. 233), who proves to be another proud and haughty nymph; and finally two more sisters (whose relationship is given): "The charming O--ds are my pleasing Theme" (l. 257). After lauding "the younger O--d" (l. 258) for her "lovely Blushes" and bright aurora beauty, the poet has dealt with all but one of his Fair Quakers. He is still only three-quarters of the way through his poem. The last section of about a hundred verses salutes the "Elder O--d" (l. 273). She is the supreme beauty to whom all the previous eighteen have been but ladies-in-waiting. She is the poet's heart's desire, and, notionally, the love-poem's objective.

.... As Venus rising from the liquid Plain,   277
Attended by the Nereids beauteous Train,
The beauteous Train in decent Order move,
Acknowledging the Sovereign Queen of Love....
     When great Apelles, emulous for Fame,   287
That Sea-born Goddess drew, each beauteous Dame
From ev'ry distant Part to th' Artist came,
That from their Charms he might conclude his Piece....
Had then our O--d liv'd, from her alone   292
The Painter had the Paphian Goddess drawn....

    Oh! that like W--ll--r, with such melting Lays   301
In tuneful Verse, I cou'd resound thy Praise,
The list'ning World should ring with O--d's Name,
And S--dn--y yield to her more lasting Fame.
But 'tis in vain, my Muse can ne'er aspire
To W--ll--r's Sweetness, or to G--v--lle's Fire;
Yet still attempts, altho' with feeble Wing,
To stretch her infant Pinions forth and sing;
Whilst her first Flight she dedicates to thee,
To thee, Successour of victorious G--.
In thee thy Mother's conquering Beauties dwell,
And thine (if possible) ev'n hers excel;
From her, inherent Wisdom does abide
With thee, and Vertue over all preside.
But who shall tell thy vast, thy boundless Wit....

And so on. Eventually the poet brings his outpourings to a close with a hint that he realises his state is too mean to make him an acceptable suitor for O--d's hand, and calls for heaven's blessings upon her.

The complete work is transcribed in Appendix Three, but those readers whose historical antennae have been set a-twirl by the cryptic clues in *The Fair Quakers* may find useful the tabulation in Appendix One of this paper. The present writer lays no great claim to be a Quaker historian; nor does he want to spoil the fun. He leaves the game of the names to others. What he will do is to explore further the background of *The Fair Quakers* and the circumstances in which it may have come to be written.

The first question, on the answer to which all else depends, is this: how reliable is the poem's claim to a Quaker connection? Three different possibilities come to mind.

The first must be that this piece was a spoof, merely one of the not-infrequent satires on Friends which were written during the late seventeenth and early eighteenth centuries. Were this to be the case, however, one would not expect to find a satire, especially one written in 1713, to be so unexpectedly appreciative. A spoof would surely be more caustic, expressing some sense of ridicule if not scorn.

Once we can accept this poem's hyperbole as being appropriate to its quasi-epic form, any shadow of satire is hard to detect. If the intention really was ironic, the irony would seem to be too subtle to achieve its object. Certainly poor Defoe was put in the pillory for the gullibility with which his satire in *The Shortest Way with the Dissenters* had been received only ten years or so before Bingley's piece came out. But there is no bite in *The Fair Quakers*. Can it really have been written with the tongue in the cheek — even for the purpose of gentle teasing rather than derision? Though not impossible, any such motivation is hard to detect. In any case, if *The Fair Quakers* was a hoax, our investigation stops here and now. Let's give it the benefit of the doubt.

The second possibility for an association with Quakerism is as a means of trade-promotion. This is not to suggest that Quakers themselves offered the poem as an advertisement for their observance, though indeed it could stand as such in some respects. Rather, the poem could have been composed by someone not a Quaker as an exercise in limbo, and then given a Quaker implant in its title and foreword as an aid to sales upon publication.

There are examples of such a practice at this period, in which the Quaker element is fabricated and tenuous. Quakers were considered by the world as beings apart. Their doings held the germ of sensational interest. Writers and publishers made fallacious use of this trend to attract customers. An instance of this is a ballad-opera by an actor of the day, Thomas Walker, entitled *The Quaker's Opera* (1728). This is devoted to the exploits of the prison-breaking robber, Jack Sheppard. Its Quaker element is essentially limited to a brief and unlikely prelude purporting to explain how the play came to be written by a Quaker's errant son. The real author, surprisingly to us today, seems to have thought that a title with "Quaker" in it would catch the public's interest better than one naming the renowned rogue-hero. In like case, therefore, the association of *The Fair Quakers* with Friends may be fictional, put there for marketing purposes. The girls may be entirely other, or may be entirely imaginary. As the only categorical statement of connection lies in the title and the verse-foreword by "R.S.", the possibility of contrivance cannot be totally ruled out.

Against this is the persuasion that the verse-foreword, the abbreviated names, and the circumstantial details (such as there are) do ring true. Today we may not know the families for which these sets of initials seem to stand, or not without much biographical research yet to be undertaken. In 1713 their interpretation would have been much easier. The contemporary reaction of Josiah Martin may be significant. As we shall see, his *Remarks*, written in response to *The Fair Quakers*, offer criticisms of the poem but nowhere deny the eponymy.

So we come to the third possibility for the origins of this poem: that the Quaker connection is valid. We are still in muddy waters. Should these girls be genuine Quaker girls, including the adored but unattainable O--d at the climax of the procession, it is to be inferred from the writer's familiarity with them that he himself was a Friend or attender, or at least an associate of some kind. It would then seem to be at odds with the Quaker norms of the time, if not altogether too creaturely, for a young Friend or even a companion not in membership to write of the girls of Meeting with such luxuriance.

We had better try a hypothesis. We have a youth, Quaker or hanger-on, despairingly in love with an unresponsive Quaker girl. If not actually a Friend or attender himself, could he be in some sort of scholarly relationship with one or another circle or family of Friends? — for he happens to be an educated young man. He is well grounded in literature, presumably accustomed from his schooling to trying his hand at formal compositions. He assuages his heart with a long love-poem. Her attractive friends underpin and set off the one he loves; he sketches them in before dwelling on her crowning charms. He wishes to please the one by pleasing the many. Who knows (ah, foolish dream), the love-poem may even sway her heart in his direction. A fair copy goes to the Adored. It goes the round of the Beauteous Train. It gets talked about. By accident or design a copy gets to a publisher's hands. John Bingley may truly not have intended the poem for public circulation, but the harm is done. For once, the publisher's disclaimer about the author's lack of involvement with the press may be meant at face value. A title is set on the piece, an introductory stanza written by a celebrity, the names in the text discreetly rendered covert, the thing is printed and is put on sale. — Well, it's a scenario.

So let us assume that *The Fair Quakers* does embody some real-life grouping of pretty young Friends. Do they belong to a single Preparative or Monthly or Quarterly Meeting? Or perhaps, every one a lily, in Lamb's famous description from his essay on "A Quakers' Meeting", are they gathering for "their Whitsun-conferences, whitening the easterly streets of the metropolis, from all parts of the United Kingdom" — where they present themselves to Bingley, as, later, to Lamb, "like troops of the Shining Ones"?

Mind, like Bunyan's original Shining Ones themselves, the generalised nature of the descriptions of the Fair Quakers makes them seem a bit disembodied. The girls are admired with great fervour but not much real differentiation. Physical descriptions are avoided, apart from dazzling eyes or a rosy complexion. Few quirks of personality or background are given, though just sufficient are hinted at to be tantalising. If Bingley was treating of real girls, and Friends at that, he may have restricted himself to generalisation because he was already stretching Quaker plainness up to and beyond acceptable bounds. So no colour of hair nor eyes, no necks nor ears nor ankles, no hands nor lips, no waists. The late Anna seems to have offered her partner N--n the "various transports of her downy breast", l. 206, but this quiver of boldness is exceptional. Elsewhere, bosoms are figurative, generally those of young men harbouring adoration. Of the living girls, "graceful her shape" is the nearest we get to anatomy.

Chapter Two

The Opinions of a contemporary Friend, Josiah Martin, in his tract "Remarks".

Whether or not the poem was approved by young female Friends in 1713, we can be sure that it was objected to by their elders, and their Elders. And whether or not *The Fair Quakers* had a basis in reality, it made at least one real-life Quaker sit up.

Josiah Martin (1685-1748) was a member of London's Peel Meeting, according to his entry in the peerless *Dictionary of Quaker Biography* at Friends' House Library. He was a scholar, a classicist, a tractarian and author of Quaker apologetics. Amongst the writers on whose work he expounded were Locke, Fénélon and Voltaire. His library is said in his will to have numbered 4,000 volumes. While many of these were no doubt pamphlets and other slight pieces, this is still a lot of books. Apparently he remained unmarried, so perhaps his books were his family. Such a large collection must have been very wide-ranging, very far from being restricted to religious studies alone.

The evidence is of him as a man of culture, of broad sympathies, and yet with his Quaker heart in the right place, as witnessed by a tract of his in 1717, *A Vindication of Women's Preaching*. At the age of 28 he was a representative of London Quarterly Meeting to the Yearly Meeting of 1714. His career as a writer seems to have taken off in this same year with these *Remarks on a Poem, intitled 'The Fair Quakers', in a Conference between Hilary and Theophilus*. This had no author's name,

11

but was shown to be printed by "Ph. Gwillim" and published by the same bookseller, Joseph Morphew, as had put out *The Fair Quakers* in 1713. The copy of *Remarks* in Friends' House Library is marked with Josiah Martin's name added by hand as the author. Before it was published, he presented his manuscript for approval to Second Day Morning Meeting. The minute reads:

> 16th 9mo 1713. Read a MS of Josiah Martins being Remarks upon a Lisentious poem, — Entituled, The Fair Quakers, and markt some Passages therein.

Tabitha Driver, of Friends' House Library, to whom I am indebted for drawing the tract and minute to my attention, suggests that the passages "markt" were to be revised. With revisions presumably in place, the tract was published by Morphew in 1714, price 2d. a copy. (That is, about equivalent to the price of a glossy magazine in modern terms).

After a prose (and prosy) preamble, Josiah Martin's *Remarks* are in the form of a dialogue, in 22 pages and not far short of 4,000 words, commencing thus:

HILARY: How do'st do, Theophilus? Hast thou seen the New Poem on the Fair Quakers?
THEOPHILUS: Yes, Hilary, I have both seen and read it.
HIL: What is thy Opinion of it? Is it not a very Ingenious Poem?
THEO: I do not at all like it.
HIL: Pray what hast thou against it?
THEO: I think it is a very Licentious and Heathenish Poem.
HIL: That is Strange! I do not see any Liberty there, more than Poets sometimes take.... How dost thou make it out to be Heathenish, Theophilus?
THEO: Very easily; instead of imploring Divine Aid, the writer of this Poem calls upon the Nymphs and Pagan Gods to assist him, and compares his Fair Ones to their Goddesses.... Then again, his Stile, and Allusions to the Fictions of the Heathen Poets, make it rank Heathenism.
HIL: Thou art too severe, Theophilus, those are only Poetick Licences.
THEO: I know of no such Licences to be met with in the Christian Poets of Apostolick Times, nor in several Ages after....
HIL: But allowance is to be made, according to the Subject; theirs being Divine, but this Juvenile and Gay.... What then, must nothing of Poetry appear abroad, but what is written in a Divine Strain?

THEO: I do not say so; but I think a Christian Author is bound to make the Glory of God, or Good of his Neighbour, the end of his Writing.

HIL: If the end of Writing were only to raise an Innocent Cheerfulness, it might in some sense be said to contribute to a Person's Good; and I am inclin'd to think, the Author of this Poem meant no worse.

THEO: I have good Will to the Author, whoever he be, and so much Charity as to think, he meant only to Please and Divert by his Poem; But when I consider the Nature of the Thing, and the Manner it is wrote in, and that 'tis now made Publick, I am griev'd to consider the Evil Consequence of it.

[Appx.4, pp 57-8; *passim*]

The effect is of a youth and his preceptor. Hilary starts off by admiring *The Fair Quakers.* Zealous though Theophilus is in countering Hilary's approval of the poem, he seems to be at pains to avoid being unfair to its author. We note that it is not only the nature and manner of the poem but also the fact that it is "now made Publick" that cause disapprobation. Is there a sense here that the poem was known to have first circulated in manuscript, but that *now* it is public it has to be (publicly) condemned?

During the course of the dialogue, the socratic method is transparent. The logic, it has to be said, is less so. Josiah Martin's discourse is entwined around two main propositions, which may be analysed as follows. The first proposition rests on objections to the paganism of the classical mythology that Bingley called upon. Theophilus has no objection to the ancients as such, writing before the Christian era, or at least not to those who were "wise heathens", exhibiting a life of moderation and self-denial. Christians, who have the example and words of Christ to follow, should avoid the "heathen style" because their purpose in writing ought to be for the benefit of mankind through the revealed glory of God. The second proposition rests on the need for establishing a life of Christian virtue. Theophilus produces arguments (with exemplars) to suggest that the poem will inflame the passions and by flattery lead to pride, thence to injustice and loss of wisdom, thence to the supremacy of the senses over the intellect, and finally to immorality — which is identified as "tending to the ruin of civil society".

In his peroration Theophilus puts a good Quaker case:

> We may now wind up the Argument, having made it appear, that Mankind derive their Happiness from Humility, and their Evils from Pride; and that Wisdom is to be obtain'd by no other way, than that of Self-denial, and taking up the Daily Cross; I mean, that Wisdom which cometh from above, which is first Pure, then Peaceable, Gentle, and easy to be entreated, full of Mercy and good Works, without Partiality, and without Hypocrisy.
>
> [Appx.4, p.64]

Hilary is safely won round to Theophilus's point of view. At the end, both speakers expatiate on the joys of Christian salvation. Hilary is even given a flight of fancy that, *mutatis mutandis*, echoes Bingley's *modus operandi:*

> HIL: O the Beauty! O the loveliness of a Humble Soul! How am I delighted with the Idea which is now presented to my Mind? Methinks I see Drusilla, at her Publick Devotion, strowing the Floor with her Tears, like Mary at the Feet of Jesus.... Oh that we had more such Humble and Contrite Souls among us! How would they Honour their Profession? Triphosa, Meek and Patient Triphosa, comes in my view: O how lovely, how Taking is her Deportment! How Condescending to her Parents! How loving, Sweet and Engaging to her Brothers and Sisters, and to all her Friends! When I have beheld her in Company, I have said in my Heart, what so Beautiful, what so Attracting as the Soul tinctured with Truth!   [Appx.4, pp 64-5]

To personalise his two ideal girls, Hilary has had to find names for them. He avoids Bingley's initialising, goes to the New Testament, and chooses a pair of names that actually have a strong Roman resonance. Drusilla was the wife of the Roman Governor Felix, Triphosa one of those remembered by Paul in his *Epistle to the Romans.* These names reinforce the latinate associations of Hilary, from Hilarius, meaning blithe, not a biblical name but the name of Roman Christian bishops, and Theophilus, "beloved of God", the addressee of *Luke* and the *Acts.* The effect may be meant to be ironic, or it may be a harmonious coincidence, in that Josiah Martin disputes with John Bingley on the latter's own cultural ground of the classical age and turns the tables on him with a Christian as against a pagan ambience.

This tract contains no refutation of the Fair Quakers as Quaker girls – it seems to accept them as such. Although there is a reference to "the author, whoever he be", Theophilus goes on to say "My intention is not to condemn the Author". One wonders if the author (anonymous at this date) was, in fact, known to Josiah Martin or at least known to be a Friend. Or perhaps the cryptically-initialled girls were recognisable. In terms of personalities, the tract pulls its punches. No denial is made of the Quaker roots claimed in the poem's preamble. In the tract there is an attempt by Hilary, admittedly overthrown, to excuse the poet and see some virtue, or at least lack of vice, in his work. Josiah Martin's desire through his protagonist Theophilus appears to be to teach a lesson, as if correcting the misguided, rather than to wound unmercifully as if attacking the avowedly hostile. Whether personal knowledge came into the matter or not, the *Remarks* accept the poem as well-meaning, not cynical. Dangerous it is thought to be, naturally, not least because the poem does not "give the Persons described a just or true Sight of Themselves,... it Flatters them abominably," and tends to "blind the Eye, to puff up the Mind, and so leads to Pride...." (Appx.4, p.60). Is there not an unspoken assumption here of the existence of "the Persons described"? That would still not prove them to be Quaker girls, in itself, but taken with Josiah Martin's silence on the issue of Quaker provenance it becomes suggestive.

Before we pass on from Josiah Martin's *Remarks* (given in full in Appendix Four), it may be that those interested in early Quaker history could find his tenor intriguing in a wider context than that of Bingley's poem merely. The preamble to the dialogue seems more pontifical in style than the dialogue itself. Those reading it may wonder if it embodies corrections "marked" by the censorship-panel of Second Day Morning Meeting by which Martin had to get his piece approved before publication. There are some heavy-handed moments in the discourse, but by and large it strikes a more restrained note than many of the Quaker pamphlets of the period. Those were, in the main, the evangelical proclamations or fierce rebuttals of criticism by a religious sect not long out of civic jeopardy and still hotly engaged in justifying itself. Apart from brief and usually dismissive generalisations, such writing had little time for any examination of artistic attitudes, which is our loss as *The Fair Quakers* was a love poem and surely never intended as a religious one. However, revealing himself as a man of culture as well of religion, Josiah Martin demonstrates the response of an early Friend to humane literature. Taken in partnership with its discussion of the attractions as well as the dangers of *The Fair Quakers*, the tract has a historical significance which transcends that of its connection with the poem alone.

15

Chapter Three

A second edition of "The Fair Quakers",
including the poem "A Funeral Elegy".

In the next year the poet disclosed himself. A second edition of *The Fair Quaker[s]* was published in 1715, with a new title-page and an additional poem.

The title-page reads:

THE FAIR QUAKER / OR The / Seraphick Amours / of / *JOHN BINGLEY* / WITH A / FEMALE FRIEND / AND HIS / Poetical LAMENTATION / Just Before his DEATH. / To which is prefix'd / his Funeral Elegy. / [bar] *By a Lover of Truth* / [bar] LONDON.... 1715 /
Price Six Pence.

We see from this that the main poem is now to be promoted with greater attention to the one Female Friend, newly isolated on the title-page in the singular as The Fair Quaker (though the plural is restored in the heading to the text of the poem); and that there is greater attention to the poet's rejection by his beloved, which inspires the closing "Lamentation". The rejection and broken heart had certainly been hinted at in the passage now dignified as "Lamentation" towards the end of the main poem, though they are not a dominant theme. The reason why the new title-page gives this emphasis is to introduce and reinforce the additional poem in 110 lines, the *Funeral Elegy*.

17

This is "prefix'd". As a new work it takes precedence in the new edition, despite the incongruity of being placed in the wrong chronological order. It is of course not a preliminary but a sequel to *The Fair Quakers*.

If Bingley exercised restraint in his first poem, in the second the author goes over the top. It is directed entirely against the "O--d" girl's cruel behaviour for scorning Bingley's addresses. Unlike *The Fair Quakers*, written in the first person, the new piece is written in the third person under the text-heading of *A Funeral Elegy on the Death of John Bingley*. It is in the same pseudo-classical style as the former piece, but in tone has a bitterness, even a savagery, absent from the other. It can be abstracted quite briefly.

> No longer Muse, no longer take thy Flights,   [l. 1
> In pleasing Strains of Love and Soft Delights;
> But...
>   ...Baleful Cypress twine about thy Brows.
> Thus Mourn the Dear Departed Celadon,
> Parnassus' Bride, and Phoebus' Darling Son....
>
> Ye Lovely Virgins, whose deserved Worth   11
> He whilome sweetly sung, and warbled forth;
> Come pay your grateful Tribute at his Urn!
> And share my Griefs; with me Lament and Mourn....
> Let flowing Tears, like boundless Nile, arise!   29
> And weep a briny Deluge from your Eyes!....
>
> In soft Tranquillity he led his Life,   34
> From Sorrow free, and from corroding Grief:...
>   ... till an envenom'd Dart,   38
> From O—d's Eyes, inflam'd his Gentle Heart....
> Long did the Bleeding Youth his Flame conceal,   43
> Afraid his hopeless Passion to reveal....
> Since therefore Silence did his Woes augment,   50
> At last, in Melting Lays, he gave his Passion vent.
>
> But, O ye Pow'rs! with what Aetherial Fire
> And Godlike Skill he struck th' Entrancing Lyre!...
> No word throughout his Theme can find a Place   61
> To stain, with rosy Dye, the purest Face....
>
> Here did the wounded Swain disclose his Grief,...   67
> That 'twou'd have mollified a Heart of Flint,...   69
> Had not his ardent Flame to One been bold,   71

18

Whose Favour only cou'd be gain'd with Gold,
Accursed Gold! to whose Imperial Sway,
Our Modern Nymphs such Adorations pay....
'Twas this that caus'd the Cruel Maid to hear   77
His Suit with Scorn, and Slight his humblest Pray'r.

    The Youth astonished stood at such Disdain....
Each setting Sun left him o'erwhelmed with Grief,   83
Nor the returning Light could yield Relief.
But more and more his poinant Pain encreas'd,...
And threw him in the cold embrace of Death!...   90
Interr'd in Dust his Body does remain: 102
Tho' no ambitious Pyramid rehearse
His Memory: yet his Immortal Verse
Shall raise a Monument, that will surpass
Or Parian Marble, or Corinthian Brass:
Which...
Fixt on the Pillars of enduring Fame   109
Shall to Eternity preserve his Name.

Regrettable exaggeration. A kind of eternity, to be immured
in the bowels of libraries for forgotten centuries. And another
ambiguity. The *Funeral Elegy* is written about John Bingley by
"a Lover of Truth". So is the author someone else, not Bingley?
Or is this a device? — offered to preserve the fiction that some
other author now writes of Bingley, who is supposed to be dead
of a broken heart, whereas in actuality Bingley is the author
again, alive and of a surety kicking? It could be either; or it
could be Bingley writing with a collaborator. It hardly matters.
The result is a hack-exercise riddled worse than ever with stylistic
clichés, clearly not to be taken as more than an exorbitant
outburst. Its unpleasing air of the sulks and self-regard is
compounded by our knowledge that in *The Fair Quakers* Bingley
had graciously accepted that his suit had little or no chance. In
lines described but not quoted before, in the main poem he had
said:

    Nor dare I once presume to hope for Ease.   361
Unhappy as I am, my wayward Fate
Has plac'd me in too low, too mean a State;
My hapless Passion makes me pine away....
Yet I in Silence will resign my Breath,   366
No Trouble shall my saucy Flame bequeath
To the lov'd Fair, whom I will bless in Death.

19

And oh! ye Powers! whate'er my Lot may prove,
On her show'r all your Blessings from Above:
Still may her Hours dance on with smiling Joy,
Free from corroding Grief's unkind Alloy....

In this light, the youth of the *Elegy* has no right to stand "astonished" at being rebuffed. The rancorous treatment of "the Cruel Maid" is a volte-face. However, we do not look for sweet reason in affairs of the heart, especially when they turn sour, and when expressed in a conventional dirge of little merit.

Nonetheless the *Funeral Elegy* has a place in the sequence of events that should not be passed over. The Quaker association is maintained via the new edition's title page. The text of the *Elegy* harks back to the earlier *Fair Quakers*, describing the poet's achievement in that poem most glowingly, and figuring the same leading lady, though no longer a lass unparalleled. If there is any real-life context behind this second piece, we readers, grown wise with our years, know that O--d's apparently mercenary dismissal of Bingley may have been the girl's excuse to be rid of an unwelcome swain, or a development compelled by an authoritative father for any one of a number of reasons, including the possibility that the poet was not in membership and that O--d would be discouraged from marrying out. So envenomed is the attack in the *Elegy* on the once-Golden Girl now turned gold-digger that we are persuaded to think that if this were a real situation she did well to escape. There is no overt reference to Quakerism beyond the continuities mentioned above. The situation of the sequel is fanciful, far more so than in the first poem; it smacks of a come-on for the market and a cheap one at that. Far from weeping a briny deluge from our eyes, let us avert them and not give this jobbery more weight than it deserves.

The *Funeral Elegy* is such an inconsiderable piece that we are led to wonder why it was ever made public, even as a corollary to promoting *The Fair Quakers* in a new edition — and especially at the swollen price of sixpence. The practices of the publishing and bookselling trade may throw some light on this.

Chapter Four

Publishing in the early 1700s and the questionable identity of "R.S."

The bookseller-publisher Joseph Morphew put out the first edition of *The Fair Quakers* in 1713, with his name on the title-page accompanied by his trade address "near Stationers Hall". Morphew also published Josiah Martin's *Remarks* in 1714. Let us remind ourselves that the second edition of *The Fair Quakers* came out in 1715, with the additional piece of *A Funeral Elegy*. The two copies of the second edition of *The Fair Quakers* that have been consulted for this paper were not published by Morphew but by two others. One copy was put out by Bernard Lintot, prolific and enterprising, one of the foremost book-trade figures of the day. This copy is in the British Library. In it, following the prefixed *Funeral Elegy*, the main poem is an exact facsimile of Morphew's first edition even to the inclusion of the original publisher's 1713 preambles. The other copy of the second edition is in Friends' House Library and was published by R. Burleigh. This copy contains only the two poems, the main work again being a facsimile of the first edition but without the preambles.

These circumstances suggest a loose association of the bookseller-publishers. This was normal at the time, though the familiar practice was for all in association to put their names to the title-page of a book they published in concert. Joseph Morphew, who so far as present information goes was the sole publisher of the first edition, was a known figure and quite capable of taking a risk-venture of his own with the first edition of *The Fair Quakers* — if risk-venture it was. More important is to note the appearance of the dominant Bernard Lintot.

It may be significant that shortly before the first appearance of *The Fair Quakers*, two major poems inspired by the epic style had been published to instant acclaim, both by Alexander Pope. His *Essay on Criticism* in verse-form came out in 1711, an extraordinary achievement for a young man of 23, and his "Rape of the Lock" was included in Lintot's *Miscellany* of 1712. In 1714 an enlarged edition of *The Rape of the Lock* was put on the market, just before the year (1715) when, eagerly awaited by the subscribers, Pope's translations of Homer were to start appearing. Pope was the most brilliant of a flock of writers who were all pushing verse in the years 1711-15. They included Prior, Gay, Swift, Rowe, Lady Mary Wortley Montagu, the Countess of Winchelsea, Thomas Parnell, Thomas Tickell, Edward ("Night Thoughts") Young, and many more beside who contributed occasional pieces to miscellanies and periodicals and whose names are now forgotten if they were ever known. They often wrote with a focus on the classical model. Like Pope himself, they used it sometimes for inspiration, sometimes for parody.

Poetry was marketable. It was in this climate that Morphew, either alone or with others, put out the first edition of the classically-grounded *Fair Quakers* in 1713, and then that Lintot, with Burleigh if no other, took it over and published the second edition in 1715, it being a piece readily to hand in the fashionable style. To tempt the market further for the reprint, the new elegaic piece was cobbled together to go with it. The appearance in 1714 of Josiah Martin's *Remarks* can only have helped, by arousing a little bubble of controversial interest and further strengthening the decision to put out the second edition of *The Fair Quakers*. When we look at these dates set out in a table, we should remember that the calendar was still old style, and that the new year began in March then, in England:

1711: Pope's *Essay on Criticism* published.
1712: Pope's "Rape of the Lock" first published in Lintot's *Miscellany.*
1713 (spring?): *The Fair Quakers* first published by Morphew, with preface by "R. S."
1713 (16 Nov*): Josiah Martin presents MS *Remarks on... 'The Fair Quakers'* read by Second-Day Morning Meeting. [* 16 "9mo.", i.e. November, O/S]
1713: Tonson's *Poetical Miscellanies*, edited by Steele, amongst other verse published this year.
1714: Josiah Martin's *Remarks on... 'The Fair Quakers'* published by Morphew (price 2d.).
1714: Pope's *Rape of the Lock* re-issued in an enlarged edition. (Further poetry published this year includes Gay's *Shepherd's Week*, Young's *Force of Religion*, Lady Winchelsea's *Miscellany Poems*.)
1715: *The Fair Quakers* re-issued by Lintot and Burleigh as *The Fair Quaker*, assigned to John Bingley as author, and accompanied by *Funeral Elegy* (price 6d.).
1715: First volume of Pope's *Homer* also published.

Our preoccupation with these resounding literary occasions will excuse our sparing but little attention for the lesser mundane events at this time of the Royal Succession crisis, the ending of the Stuart monarchy with the death of Queen Anne in August 1714, the arrival of the House of Hanover with the accession of George I, and the Jacobite rebellion of 1715. We do take heed of the minor involvement in those affairs of one particular man of letters, Sir Richard Steele.

Steele was an important writer who was well-known for his plays, his pamphlets, and his contributions to (and sponsorship of) the great Augustan periodicals *The Tatler* (1709-11), *The Spectator* (1711-12), and *The Guardian* (March-October, 1713, essentially under Steele's own proprietorship). His reputation stood high to the middle of 1713. Then for a year he was under a cloud. As a fervent Whig, and supporter of the Hanoverian cause, he entered Parliament in mid-1713, relinquishing sinecures to do so, in order to attack the Tory government over the abandonment of the Dunkirk fortifications that followed the Treaty of Utrecht in April 1713. In early 1714 he published a pamphlet on the succession crisis which was so hard-hitting that he was expelled the House for sedition. From this slide downwards he was rescued by the accession of George I, who was crowned in October 1714 when he finally came over to claim his throne. In 1715 Steele's fortunes swung right up again. For his pains on behalf of the new monarch, Steele was made a Justice of the Peace, Deputy-Lieutenant of Middlesex, Surveyor of the Royal Stables, Proprietor of the King's Comedians (that is, boss of Drury Lane Theatre), and a knight of the realm; and after the suppression of the Jacobite rebellion he was appointed a commissioner of forfeited estates. So we can see that up to the first half of 1713, Steele's name had been one to be reckoned with. He was a man both of letters and affairs, the type out of whom you might try to get a foreword, for example, if you were a publisher promoting an unknown writer. Then for a year or so his political partisanship and parliamentary suspension made him a bit too much of a hot potato, until in 1715 the royal favour so revived his fame and fortunes that, from being a hot potato, he became once again a hot property.

Richard Steele's initials are R. S. These initials appear at the foot of the verse-foreword that is printed in Morphew's first edition of *The Fair Quakers.* The verses and initials are repeated in Lintot's second edition despite Bingley's name being given to it as the author, thus contradicting the verse-foreword's hailing of the author as an "unknown youth". It looks as though Lintot took over the formes of the first edition and re-printed the lot (including the misprints, e.g. "of" for "or" in line 374), regardless of the authorial inconsistency. Burleigh, the other publisher of the second edition, was more careful. He removed the preambles referring to the author's anonymity, now that Bingley's name appeared on the title-page.

So was this illogically-treated verse-foreword by "R.S." actually written by Richard Steele? In 1713, still of high repute, was he approached for a small hack commission here — or did he, perhaps, contribute the foreword out of charity? It is on record that Steele had a publishing relationship with Lintot; and there was some kind of connection between Lintot and Morphew. We also know that Steele wrote kindly of Quakers in papers now attributed to him, namely *The Tatler* no. 204 (1710) and *The Spectator* no. 132 (1711). Although impulsive and profligate, Steele was a generous man, and, like his co-essayist Addison, a humane moralist.

One of his *Guardian* essays of 1713 is worth quoting here — an essay that, if not written by Steele himself, came out under his imprimatur. The "Guardian" speaks of poetic composition and courtship, in the voice of "Nestor Ironside", elder and sage:

> An agreeable young gentleman, that had a talent for poetry, and does me the favour to entertain me with his performances after my more serious studies, read me yesterday the following translation... *[namely a passage from Claudian, part of the Epithalamium on Honorius and Maria].* In this town,... I am very glad when I gain so much time of reflection from a youth... as is taken up in any composition, tho' the piece he writes is not foreign to... his natural inclination. For it is a great step towards gaining upon the passions, that there is a delicacy in the choice of their object; and to turn the imaginations towards a bride, rather than a mistress, is getting a great way towards being in the interests of virtue. It is a hopeless manner of reclaiming youth,... to declaim against pleasure in general: No; the way is to shew, that the pleasurable course is that which is limited and governed by reason.... I have for this reason often thought of exercising my pupils, of whom I have several of admirable talents, upon writing... compositions [which] should be written on the little advances made towards a young lady of the strictest virtue, and all the circumstances alluded to in them, should have something that might please her mind in its purest innocence, as well as celebrate her person in its highest beauty.
>
> (*The Guardian* no. 127, 6 Aug. 1713)

Writing a supportive foreword to *The Fair Quakers* would have been consistent with the ideas here expressed, and consistent with what we know of Richard Steele.

The reappearance of the foreword signed by R.S. in Lintot's second edition of *The Fair Quakers* corroborates the presumption that Steele was the "R.S." concerned. Lintot is unlikely to have given a by-line to any R. S. other than Richard Steele. What is more, Lintot's desire to include an introductory contribution that he knew was by Steele, an author re-ascendant in 1715 as we have seen, may be the reason why he retained the original preambles in his second edition despite the awkwardness over naming the author. Burleigh, the other publisher of second-edition copy, removed the awkward preambles, and was the better bibliographer; Lintot ignored the awkwardness, and went for sales supported by his inclusion of a stanza by the illustrious "R.S.".

Chapter Five

A possible scenario for John Bingley.

Though Sir Richard Steele is a much more interesting character than anyone else in our purview, we have to tear ourselves away from him in order to ask, finally, what of John Bingley?

This may be the real name of a young man with no more than the slightest of links with Friends, an admirer from some distance of the Society's young lilies. Alternatively the author of *The Fair Quakers* may have been in close association with the Society, even in membership. Though it is true that the author may have been writing under a pseudonym, Bingley is not an unfamiliar name in Quaker annals. The Birmingham Lloyds (of Lloyd's Bank) lived in "Bingley Hall". More germane is a weighty Friend who came to prominence in the seventeenth century, William Bingley (1651-1715), who removed from Yorkshire to London, where he was living by 1682. He was a notable travelling and writing Friend, and was one of those who gave ministry at the funeral of George Fox. The *Dictionary of Quaker Biography*, whence these details, is silent about any issue or other relatives that he may have had. We do not know what connection other than the coincidence of a surname there may be between weighty William Bingley and romantic John Bingley, as research stands at the moment. Nevertheless we have enough here to recapitulate our earlier scenario and hazard its completion.

There is a Quaker family of Bingleys, in London, of which, say, William Bingley (born 1651) is the paterfamilias. Comes the dawn of the eighteenth century, and Queen Anne's "Augustan Age". A young sprig of the Bingley tribe, John, shows parts. A good education is contrived for him. He gets captivated by the classical poets, and by the recent English masters: for Dryden's exhaustive renderings of the ancients — Virgil, Ovid, Homer — had come out in the 1690s, and Pope's *Pastorals* made their mark in 1709. Dryden and Pope were but the two best of many composers at this time of the heroic couplet in the classical style. Under their spell young Bingley practises his own way with verse. His circle seems to include many Quaker maidens; one or two also try their hand at writing. We ponder again the likelihood of their being in some kind of group-relationship through Meeting or their families, perhaps even a scholarly one. Round about the year 1712, being under the spell of a particular Fair Quaker as well as his literary mentors, in her honour John Bingley puts himself to an exuberant exercise of the tricks of the poetic trade.

He enjoys himself, exploiting his new-learnt scholarship regardless of clichés, perhaps even unaware of them. He delights in his routine manipulation of rhythm and rhyme and rhetorical rules, at which we raise an amused if tolerant eyebrow. He flaunts his familiarity with the best-known figures of classical mythology. His joyousness is all the greater for his subject being young women, and one in particular, thus legitimising his abiding day-dream. At the same time he is nice-minded. He keeps what he says about the girls within bounds. One or two of them, supposing that they were real girls whom he knew, might have tossed their heads over an adverse comment on their unkindness to their swains, but his prevailing attitudes are esteem and respect. He is well brought up, a young lover with virtuous instincts. It is all too possible to see the same youth's revulsion against such instincts in the disappointment that led to the *Funeral Elegy*. Viewed without prejudice today, *The Fair Quakers* has a propriety, Hilary's "innocent cheerfulness", that is not to be denied.

Bingley's writing is powerfully derivative, not powerfully imaginative. If his verse is conventional, at least it flows smoothly. It is clear from his love-poem that he is a cultivated youth. Perhaps, though, he is a younger son or otherwise without expectations, because his "too low, too mean a state" seems to make his love unlikely to prosper. He says that he has been a stranger till now to the power of the God of Love, and indicates that this poem is his muse's "first flight". These deprecations may be assumed, or truly part of a lover's heart-ache.

Let us continue to imagine that once *The Fair Quakers* has been circulated, John Bingley suffers reverses. His family, perhaps the girl's family and others, admonish him. Visitation from an Elder is on the cards, for John to be "spoken to" (so the minute would be phrased: dread prospect). He is made fully aware of the disparagement with which the publication of his labour of love is received amongst Friends. One London Friend, Josiah Martin, belabours him in print for his "licentious" poem, perhaps as one Quaker to another, and not without some understanding of the genre and an avowal "not to condemn the author". Bruised by Martin's *Remarks* Bingley nonetheless remains. Though we can find it in us to hope that some of the eighteen attendant Fair Quakers manage to whisper a sweet word of comfort to him, the nineteenth stays aloof. The bitterest outcome of all is to have his love rejected by the heroine when his approach becomes known, for he had deluded himself that the poem in which he had invested such effort and such hope might yet weigh with her.

All this could follow from the publication of *The Fair Quakers* in 1713 and the *Remarks* in 1714. To it all John Bingley, in the heat of his youth, reacts adversely. He feels disillusioned, humiliated, resentful. His adherence to the Society of Friends is under strain, and might give way if it were not for the strong hand of paterfamilias William Bingley. Then William Bingley's hand weakens.

Concurrently with William Bingley's approach to death in 1715 comes news that *The Fair Quakers* is to be re-issued. Will John Bingley write a companion-piece? Perhaps he does; perhaps someone else writes the *Funeral Elegy*, splenetic sequel to the poem that had originally been penned with such generosity of spirit and then so comprehensively spurned. At least let the world know his name. So authorship of *The Fair Quakers* is ascribed to John Bingley in the reprint.

He is heard of no more. We take his death of a broken heart, as the *Elegy* would have it, with a large handful of salt. It is possible, of course, that he did die at that time, from some other cause. Failing this, what is the reason for his subsequent silence, his exit from the records? Did he break away from the Society of Friends?

Pure speculation. Many alternative case-studies are possible, including the one that there is no case to start with. How solemn our enquiry — but what high jinks we have had along the way. And how tempting it is, in weighing the manifold pros and cons, to follow in Josiah Martin's footsteps, and present the argument in the form of dialogue between, say, Credulus and Criticus:

> CREDULUS: Tell me, Criticus, have you considered the possibility that "John Bingley" may have been none other than Friend Josiah Martin himself, writing secretly under a false name?
> CRITICUS: No, Credulus, because such falsity does not fit with what we know of Josiah Martin. And the professing Quakers of his time would not play such jackanape tricks, even upon the creature world....

Let us sum up before we drown in a sea of supposition.

The verse-foreword suggests itself as an item to be added to the known writings of Sir Richard Steele that are favourable to Quakers. As for *The Fair Quakers*, the existence of some contemporary interest in the poem, 1713-15, is unassailable. Its authorship by John Bingley as a young Friend or attender, or fellow-scholar of Friends' youngsters, even tutor to them, is plausible. There may be more to the poem than meets the eye, but it paints an attractive and unusual picture. Placed before the world of 1713, it is flattering to the Society of Friends, and conceivably brings before us a unique flock of Quaker maidens, otherwise collectively lost to history. For Friends themselves, Josiah Martin's *Remarks* tract of 1714 made the necessary correction of attitudes, and is valuable for presenting today's reader with a considered account of what one early eighteenth-century Friend thought acceptable in the literature of the day. The poem's coda, Bingley's supposed *Funeral Elegy, by A Lover of Truth,* defies and forfeits estimation, save that, despite the spirit of pathos which it attempts to generate, it causes us to have less sympathy with the love-lorn youth than we might have had.

The nineteen Fair Quakers and their singer remain ectoplasmic. The table of "names" (Appendix One) does its best to bring them before us by giving an abstract of such detail about individuals as the poem enables us to glean. The game of trying to give historical body to these shades is offered to readers, should any be sufficiently intrigued. It may eventually be found that the Fair Quakers have some real-life validity. If so, Bingley's plea to "let their Names immortalize my Verse" will achieve a modest prophetic value. Alternatively, the poem may revert to limbo, unsolved. For rescue's sake, and the interest of anyone minded to read the documents in full or refer to their detail, the three originals are here reprinted in the Appendices Three, Four and Five.

John Bingley may or may not have been a Quaker John Bingley, and his poem is hardly world-shaking, but the puzzle he has left behind him continues to tease.

Appendices

Appendix One

The "Names" and the Clues

Reading the poem is made more comfortable by imagining a proper name for each set of initials in turn. It is an easy matter in theory to suggest many possible names for filling out the sets of family initials, but to list some of the candidates here beyond minimum examples would be to spoil the fun. The game of seeking to identify any real historical personages behind these initials, in a grouping consistent with the stance of the poem, is offered to readers.

The features of the game can be summarised. Twenty soi-disant Quakers are mentioned, nineteen girls and one man. The initials awarded to them seem to refer to family names, that is surnames, rather than to first names, with one possible exception. The group to which these families belong may be a fixed one (Preparative Meeting, Monthly Meeting or Quarterly Meeting), or they may have come together for a conference such as Yearly Meeting. The period is circa 1712-13. Some slight hints, by no means proof, point to a base in or near London.

The names of the twenty are abbreviated to the first and last initials, some having an extra initial at the beginning or end, save for one girl now dead whose first name, Anna, is given in full; her partner is the one man initialised. Five further sets of initials refer to four people other than the twenty *dramatis personæ* and to one place-name. The number of syllables, and the position of the stress, in the abbreviated names can be deduced from scansion. Some are of one syllable, like "H--s", though most are of two syllables, like "W--n", with the stress on the first syllable, as with nearly all such English names. (Elementary, my dear W--n....) The possibility of patronymic prefixes throwing the stress on to the second syllable, like MacMahon, O'Dowd, seems to be ruled out metrically. One name is of three syllables, again with the stress on the first syllable. Not one of the names have rhymes which help with their interpretation.

The list of "names" which follows gives them in alphabetical order, with their number of syllables in brackets, and a line-reference to the name's first appearance in the text. Any clues to individuality, vague though most of these are, are then summarised.

Dramatis Personæ

B--rs (2), l. 27: a virgin "in her prime", "graceful her shape", serene and with "an unaffected smile".

C--tt (2), l. 169: cheerful, artless, like Eve before the Fall.

Ec--n (3), l. 141: the only three-syllabled name. She is "blooming, fair, and young"; graced by "maternal glories" [i.e. glories inherited from her mother?], yet a "lovely maid".

H--s (1), l. 61: "innocently gay", "affable", but denies suit being a "blushing maid".

Ma--n (2), l. 36: has "radiant eyes" that kindle. Sister of below?

A Younger Ma--n (2), l. 48: "Beaming glories crown her youthful head" [ref. to hair?]. Has "dawning charms". Kid sister of above?

M--re (1), l. 83: engaging, youthful, virtuous — "a virgin all complete".

M--s (1), l. 233: beautiful, but a disdainful "haughty nymph", who is begged not to scorn but to pity her swains.

N--n (2), l. 205: the one male. Youthful squire or spouse of the late Anna -- "happy man!" It is possible that his initials here stand for his first name, in apposition to that of Anna.

O--d (2), (l. 19 and) l. 273: the poet's heart's desire, and the end-focus of *The Fair Quakers* in which she is praised for over a hundred lines. She is "beauty's unrivalled queen", witty, wise, and virtuous; a poetess herself. She is spoken of as "successor of victorious G--". She is one in whom her "mother's conquering beauties dwell". In the later *Funeral Elegy* the tune changes: after her dismissal of the poet's approaches, she is now one "whose favour only could be gained with gold", a "Cruel Maid" who hears "his suit with scorn" because he is of "too low, too mean a state" — a bitter U-turn which need be taken at even less face-value than the encomium.

O--d (2), **the Younger**, l. 258: a mild and blushing beauty, sister of above.

O--n (2), **Anna**, l. 203: née O--n, possibly married and certainly committed to N--n. She is the one person with a fully-spelt name, in her case the first name, possibly because she is now dead. She was mild, influential; elder sister of below.

O--n (2), l. 191: "one of the loveliest of the lovely few"; charming and wise. Blessed by her elder sister Anna, above, when Anna was on her death-bed.

P--m (2), l. 97: "serenely gay"; has red and white rosy cheeks.

P--n (2), l. 71: admired, but seen as a "haughty maid", and warned that she should shed her influence "with gentler rays".

T--r (2), l. 110: dazzling, majestic, but proud and apparently on the look-out for conquests; ultimately disdainful, yet a "bright nymph". Sister of below?

A **Younger** T--r (2), l. 135: shines less fiercely than the above (her sister?), but no less pleasingly; mild, graceful, as yet heart-free.

V--s (2), l. 149: splendid and courteous; Diana-like, surrounded by maidens; has sense, wit, eloquence. There is a hint that she sings and in turn inspires "rural lays", and a hint of her being a countrywoman, perhaps only visiting — "Long may the virgin, long with us remain".

W--n (2), l. 55: there is a hint that she has suffered: adversity refines "each sundry charm"; her virtue shines "like diamonds set in jet".

W--r (2), l. 87: notable for her wit; also has sense and beauty.

Further names mentioned.

G-- (1), l. 310: rhymes with "thee". O--d is spoken of as "successor of victorious G--", so this may be an ancestor, or the first-name initial of her mother or father. The Quaker context, however, makes it equally possible that this is the initial of one whose "victorious" example O--d is held to follow, and may thus be an oblique reference to George Fox.

S--dn--y, W--ll--r, G--v--lle (all 2-syllabled names), ll. 304 and 306: these are the three lyric poets (Philip Sidney, Edmund Waller, and Fulke Greville) who are Bingley's models in his lays of love.

S--te (2), l. 119: a place-name — the only one: a refuge of groves and shade. This could be anywhere: Sandgate and Sheepcote on the south coast; Sapcote in the midlands; Seathwaite, Stonethwaite in the Fells; and so on. There are several Southgates. The Southgate between Barnet and Enfield, eight miles or so north of central London, was a wooded spot on the edge of Enfield Chase and certainly fits the requirements. With this in mind, the facts also that the poem's place of publication was London and that the critical responder (Josiah Martin) was a London Friend add up to a slight but unproven balance in favour of the base of the Fair Quakers' grouping being somewhere in London.

The authors

John Bingley. A young man, perhaps a very young man; cultivated, and keen on classical legend and on the modish poetry of his day; probably of limited means. Seems to know his Fair Quakers well enough to refer to their family relationships — sisters, a mother or two — and seems to refer to himself as belonging to their group when he says "Long may the virgin... with us remain". Starts off deeply in love with the elder O--d, but after being rebuffed appears to be in equally deep disillusionment.

A Lover of Truth. Supposed author of sequel, *A Funeral Elegy* of 1715; may be Bingley himself, or someone writing in association with Bingley or the publishers. Of little importance in relation to the Fair Quakers as people.

R. S. Author of the verse-foreword to *The Fair Quakers* in 1713. Almost certainly Sir Richard Steele.

Josiah Martin. A documented Friend, author of tract published in 1714 to rectify the poem's errors, namely *Remarks on... 'The Fair Quakers'*. Treats the poem with firmness but some generosity; does not refute the poem's claim to be inspired by Quaker girls nor the poem's right to its title. A member of Peel Meeting, London. Aged about 28 at the time of publication. Known to have had a brother John, five years younger than himself; no other sibling relatives, e.g. sisters, known to the *D.Q.B.* It may or may not be significant that two of the Fair Quakers have a family name abbreviated to "Ma--n" (two syllables).

Verse Technique

It is almost axiomatic that John Bingley's schooling brought some study of classical epic and lyric in the original. It would seem inevitable that his education or his leisure reading included the ancient authors in translation. His easy way with English and his familiarity with the superficialities of Greek mythology suggest the influence of Dryden and Pope, whose translations and imitations of Homer, Ovid, and Virgil were all the rage in the twenty years before *The Fair Quakers* was published.

Bingley's imagery is fully in the classic groove. The lyre, song, anthem, taking flight or wing are stock figures for poetic composition. There are images of jewels, of roses, of pastoral effects, but the mass of metaphor is in the heavens, the empyrean. The sun, stars, moon, clouds, storm, night and other manifestations of "th'ætherial height" constantly show up, but especially day, light, and the sun. It is tempting to think that this may relate in some way to subconscious yearnings. Otherwise the fields from which Bingley culls his metaphorical blooms are surprisingly limited. He goes outside these, though, to history and art for his most pleasing conceit, which recalls the competition for modelling Apelles's Venus Anadyomene.

The frequent classical allusions invoke the pagan culture decried by Josiah Martin. Most are stereotyped and within the mould of any retelling of the Greek myths. Strephon is a late-comer to the catalogue, deriving from Sidney's *Arcadia,* and there is a biblical reference, to Eve before the Fall. However, the mythological treatment is reasonably consistent.

Bingley knew the tricks of prosody. At least twelve alexandrines copiously occur, for emphasis or to close a period. Minor inversions of the metrical beat, so ably employed by the masters, occur all too rarely save for a standard trochaic first foot. Pauses are nearly always at line-end, though there is one Miltonic enjambement and caesura:

> "...There her Breath
> Stop'd, and she smiling sunk into the Arms of Death."

There are many elisions, mostly though not all mark'd [sic] by an apostrophe in place of the missing vowel. The articulation of the past-participular ending "-ed" was on its way out, though not yet gone for good. The actor David Garrick, fifty years after this poem, advised on the delivery of a phrase in the prayer-service as "errëd and stray'd" (thus *Theatre Notebook* xxxviii/ 1, 13). The rhymes seem pretty true to the pronunciation of the time, though with a few sounds odd to today's ear. We are not deceived by Bingley's "...enshrin'd/find/join'd", a rhyme confirmed in the extract from Pope below. No less than sixteen triplets trip it as they go amongst the heroic couplets, signified in the original text, as was normal then, by being bracketed in the margin.

As with so many other versifiers of the day, we can see whence Bingley caught his tone (though not his overkill) from a few lines of Dryden's rendering of Dido's love for Æneas (*Æneid*, IV, ll. 1-16 and 89-92):

> But anxious cares already seiz'd the queen:
> She fed within her veins a flame unseen:
> The hero's valour, acts, and birth, inspire
> Her soul with love, and fan the secret fire.
> His words, his looks, imprinted in her heart,
> Improve the passion, and increase the smart.
> Now, when the purple morn had chased away
> The dewy shadows, and restor'd the day,
> Her sister first with early care she sought,
> And thus in mournful accents eas'd her thought:
> "My dearest Anna! what new dreams affright
> My lab'ring soul! what visions of the night
> Disturb my quiet, and distract my breast
> With strange ideas of our Trojan guest!

His worth, his actions, and majestic air,
A man descended from the gods declare...."

...What priestly rites, alas! what pious art,
What vows, avail to cure a bleeding heart?
A gentle fire she feeds within her veins,
Where the soft god secure in silence reigns....

We get the feeling that John Bingley was in love with literature as well as with the elder O--d girl. He shows plenty of enthusiasm, though his creative imagination is not powerful. His verse, like his language, is conventional, all of a sameness. But he could write. His poem flows harmoniously — great work it is not, but it is smooth. Within the routine terms it sets itself, his verse is accomplished, and does the author more credit than otherwise. Morphew hoped that *The Fair Quakers* would accord well with what most readers of his time would admire. Richard Steele seems to have thought so too.

Would Pope, the master poet, have so admired? We fear not. Here are lines [ll. 337-358] from *An Essay on Criticism* that Pope published in 1711, himself only twenty-three at the time. John Bingley could have learnt from them if he had been so minded. Perhaps he did, a little:

...But most by numbers judge a Poet's song;
And smooth or rough, with them is right or wrong:...
These equal syllables alone require,
Tho' oft the ear the open vowels tire;
While expletives their feeble aid do join;
And ten low words oft creep in one dull line:
While they ring round the same unvary'd chimes,
With sure returns of still expected rhymes;
Where'er you find 'the cooling western breeze',
In the next line, it 'whispers through the trees':
If crystal streams 'with pleasing murmurs creep',
The reader's threaten'd (not in vain) with 'sleep':
Then, at the last and only couplet fraught
With some unmeaning thing they call a thought,
A needless Alexandrine ends the song
That, like a wounded snake, drags its slow length along....

Appendix Three

A copy of the 1st Edition of "The Fair Quakers" (1713)

THE PUBLISHER TO THE READER.

I am very well acquainted that the Excuses of a Friend's Importunity, or his stealing a Copy, or its having unadvisedly been distributed, and so committed privately to the Press, and the like, are so common and thread-bare, that they are grown a standing Jest: Yet, notwithstanding this, I will venture to assure the Readers of this following Poem, that this is really the Case, and that the Author of it will probably be later acquainted with the printing of it, and I am sure much more surprized than the Reader. For the truth is, I saw and was pleas'd with the Piece, which I found, in my Opinion, as well as in that of several much better Judges, to be Easy, Just, and entirely Novel. For which Reason I resolv'd without his Knowledge (whose Consent I was sure never to obtain) to thrust it into the Press: Which is the main Reason why you now find it made Publick. As for the Fate it may meet with in the World, the Author I am sure will be very little concern'd, nor I believe any one else, except the Bookseller and my self; He for his own Profit, and I, that (after this Presumption) I may look my Friend in the Face with better Assurance. So, Reader, I leave it with you, and wish you as much Pleasure in perusing it as I had.

Well, unknown Youth, hast thou thy Friends express'd,
And thy Fair Quakers like themselves hast dress'd:
Moving and soft, and gayly innocent;
Without Excess, yet full of Ornament.
Of youthful vertue thus proceed to write,
And by Example as by Verse invite.
With Innocence and Beauty grace your Strains,
The listening Isle shall bless your tuneful Pains:
Vertue resume her Sway and Vice retire,
And O--d reign, while thus she does inspire
The Friendly Muse, and guide the Quaker Lyre.

R.S.

The Fair Quakers: A Poem

A id sacred Nymphs of the *Pierian* Spring!
  While I no vulgar Theme attempt to sing.
And *Phoebus*, tuneful God, my Breast inspire,
Expand my Soul with thy Celestial Fire,
Conduct those Numbers, and direct those Lays
Which now I dedicate to Beauty's Praise.
Thy kind Assistance too, soft God of Love,
To me vouchsafe, thy Influence let me prove.
Virgins from thee derive their various Charms,
Their Eyes are thy bright Magazine of Arms: 10
And thou from them deriv'st thy Sovereign Sway,
What they command we joyfully obey.
Instruct me then their Beauties to rehearse,
And let their Names immortalize my Verse.
And tho' till now (a Stranger to thy Power)
I never did thy sacred Shrine adore,
Let Ignorance for past Neglect attone,
And spare th' unwitting Fault, because unknown.
Fair O--d now too strongly does attest
Thy potent Sway, and wounds my suff'ring Breast: 20
Thy Godhead I confess, oh! move the Fair
To hear and be propitious to my Prayer;
And thy bright Train, whilst I attempt to write,
Assist my feeble Lays and guide my infant Flight.

BEGIN, auspicious Muse, the pleasing Song,
Fir'd with new Beauties as thou go'st along.
See lovely *B--rs* first in sight appears,
A Blooming Virgin in her Prime of Years,
Graceful her Shape, delightful is her Mien,
An unaffected Smile, an Air serene   30
Adorn her Face, where growing Charms are seen;
Sweet Innocence does from each Action flow,
Whilst thronging Lovers sigh, adore and bow:
But from th' insnaring Wiles the Beauty free
Maintains with Care her native Liberty.

Ma--n, with conqu'ring charms the Soul commands,
And captive leads the Heart in willing Bands;
The sparkling Lustre of her radiant Eyes
The Lover's Breast invades with sweet Surprize.
Amaz'd to feel the soft encroaching Pain,   40
He sighs and looks, and looks and sighs again,
Which soon augmenting kindles to Desire,
And fills his glowing Breast with am'rous Fire.
Then to the Virgin wou'd his Flame disclose
To stop the Torrent of invading Woes:
But, dreading the fierce Terrors of her Frown,
Retires, and mourns his hopeless Love alone.

BEHOLD, a younger *Ma--n* comes in Sight,
Who shortly will shine forth with wond'rous Light;
Her budding Charms uncommon Lustre spread,   50
And beaming Glories crown her youthful Head.
Too soon, alas! the fatal Day shall come
Her dawning Charms shall in full Splendo[u]r bloom,
And each desiring Swain to Sighs and Anguish doom.

NOR, *W--n,* shall thy Worth unsung remain,
Misfortunes never shall thy Lustre stain,
Thy pleasing Beauties chear the ravish'd Sight,
And sooth[e] the Senses with a strange Delight;
Each sundry Charm Adversity refines,
Like Diamonds set in Jet thy Vertue shines.   60

45

YOUNG *H--s* appears, all innocently gay
Driving from ev'ry Breast Despair away;
So affable the Fair, so soft and kind,
She frees from gloomy Cares the Lover's Mind:
Yet when her tender Bosom he would move,
And to the Nymph reveal his ardent Love,
With soothing Rhet'rick wou'd her Heart persuade
To yield to the sweet Power; the Blushing Maid,
Free from th'enchanting Pain, his Suit denies,
And Innocence the Place of Pride supplies.   70

    P--n a fatal Splendour darts abroad,
Which, Comet like, sure Ruin does forebode;
Her Lovers trembling view her, and admire
The glitt'ring Cause of such destructive Fire:
They sigh, they languish, but, alas! in vain,
The haughty Maid returns it with Disdain,
Plays with their Passion, and neglects their Pain.
Fair Nymph, your Influence shed with gentler Rays,
Meteors soon vanish tho' they fiercely blaze,
Whilst milder Planets, with distinguish'd Light   80
And holy Fires, adorn the silent Night,
To distant Ages regularly bright.

    ENGAGING *M--re* appears with artless Grace,
A Thousand blooming Charms adorn her Face;
Youth and fair Vertue both in her are met,
And strive to form a Virgin all compleat.

    NEXT I advance to sing fair *W--r's* Name,
W--r whose Wit deserves immortal Fame:
Her solid Sense in Conversation gains
Applause, and captivates the listning Swains,   90
Whilst joyful they attend the pleasing Sound,
And from her Lips receive Love's powerful Wound.
Th' ingenious Sallies of her Wit engage
Passion from Youth, and kind Regard from Age;
With which resplendent Beauty does combine
To make the charming Maid conspicuous shine.

FAIR *P--m* next behold, serenely gay,
Pleasing as Summer's Shades and mild as May,
As Roses in their vernal Bloom appear,
To Sight and Smell delicious, sweet and fair,   100
Some with their Crimson Blush delight the View,
And others with their native Snowy Hue;
In *P--m's* Cheeks these Opposites unite,
The blushing Crimson and the snowy White;
So blended, neither claims Prerogative,
But from her Eyes new Glories both receive.

ATTEMPT, my Muse, attempt a loftier Strain,
But guide thy strong Career with steddy Rein,
The shining Track of Beauty swift pursue,
T--r, the dazling *T--r* comes in view.   110
Admiring Crowds around the Virgin wait,
Whilst she, majestic, walks in awful State;
And, conscious of the Lustre of her Eyes,
Darts forth their Beams some Lover to surprize.
Whose Lightening, swift as is the Heav'nly Dart,
Wounds but too soon the trembling Gazer's Heart,
Who loth her Anger, or her Scorn to prove,
Anxious, conceals the Secret of his Love.
Then to soft *S--te* Shades the Youth retires,
There, on the Barks of Trees, records his Fires: 120
And, Sorrow from his Bosom to remove,
Lov'd *T--r's* Name repeats in every Grove;
The Groves again repeat lov'd *T--r's* Name,
And the dear Sound augments his am'rous Flame.
But if o'erpress'd at length he tells his Pain,
The humble Tale she answers with Disdain.
For you, bright Charmer, *Strephon* pines away,
Pensive with heaving Sighs he spends the Day;
Yet tries his inward Passion to conceal,
But speaking Eyes the Secret will reveal: 130
The hidden Flame does on his Vitals feed,
As Wounds most dangerous are that inward bleed.
Extend, bright Nymph, some pity to the Youth,
And with a mutual Flame reward his Truth.

A YOUNGER *T--r* shines Celestial bright,
With a less fierce, but no less pleasing Light,
Her milder Features shed peculiar Grace,
Nor Pride nor Scorn her pleasing Charms deface,
And Stranger to the Tyrant Cupid's Dart,
Serene and gay appears with an unwounded Heart.　　　140

SEE *Ec--n* all blooming, fair and young,
To whom unnumber'd budding Charms belong;
Her wond'rous Beauty yields a swift Delight,
She pains at once, at once she chears the sight:
Maternal Glories grace the lovely Maid,
Glories, which Time it self can scarce invade:
Yet she by Time her Charms increas'd shall find,
And future Years will prove to Beauty kind.

TO *V--s* next direct thy Flight, my Muse,
V--s whose Charms transcendent Joys diffuse;　　　150
A daz[z]ling Splendour blazes from her Eye,
And on her Brow sits awful Majesty:
Yet her soft Mien and courteous Beauties move
Beholders, to admire at once and love:
The Fair, amidst the blushing Maidens, seems
As Chast[e] *Diana* by *Eurota's* Streams,
When she, surrounded by her Virgin Train,
Warm in the Eager Chase flies o'er the Plain.
But who shall sing her vast superiour Sense?
Her flowing Wit and pleasing Eloquence!　　　160
Such warbling Strains her tuneful Muse inspires,
She warms the neighbouring Youths with soft Desires,
And kindles in their Breasts Poetick Fires.
To her they dedicate their Rural Lays,
Whilst distant Hills resound bright *V--s'* Praise.
Long may the Virgin, long with us remain,
With her soft Lyre to cure the poignant Pain,
And chear the Heart of every drooping Swain.

YOUNG *C--tt's* Features Heav'nly Charms display,
All beautiful without the least Allay;　　　170

48

She wounds without Design each tender Breast,
And every gazing Swain deprives of Rest;
Yet tries no sly insinuating Arts
To gain a Conquest o'er unguarded Hearts;
But 'tis her Innocence the Youth insnares,
And warms his doubtful Breast with pleasing Cares:
He sighs whene'er the lovely Maid he views,
And with his longing Eyes the Fair pursues.
Whilst kindly she commiserates his Grief,
And sooth[e]s the Torment she must not relieve.   180
In her appears a graceful Negligence,
Soft chearful Smiles bedeck'd with Innocence;
Such, ere her Fall, was our first Mother *Eve*
Before the Serpent taught her to deceive,
She us'd no Bait to tempt the Man to Sin,
All perfect fair without, and spotless all within:
Her Breast for him alone with Passion burn'd,
And his alone to her the like return'd,
So may'st thou, *C--tt*, such a Lover find,
True as thy Vertues, as thy Beauties kind.   190

    O--n, the blooming *O--n*, comes in View,
One of the loveliest of the lovely Few;
More bright the Fair, than in Celestial Spheres
The Evening Star above the rest appears,
Who Eastward darts his far superiour Ray,
Retaining still some bright Remains of Day:
The smaller Sparks together all combine,
And all together far more faintly shine;
Weak languid Streams of Light from them descend,
And to our searching Sight but dimly tend;   200
Whilst *Hesp'rus* sends far more refulgent Beams,
And gilds with Streaks of Light the Chrystal Streams.
Such radiant Charms bright ANNA did dispence,
Many she chear'd with her mild Influence;
Whilst youthful *N--n*, happy Man! possess'd
The various Transports of her downy Breast,
On him alone the lovely Nymph bestow'd
The choicest Raptures of Terrest[r]ial Good;

But the bright Charmer her Seraphick Mind
To Heaven, its native Seat, too soon resign'd: 210
Yet first her pious Thoughts she thus express'd,

"On thee, Dear Sister, numerous blessings rest,
And may'st thou long enjoy a double Store
Of Comforts here, which I shall taste no more:
I now ascend to far superiour Bliss,
To lasting Transports, endless Happiness;
Where thou, thro' Wisdom's Aid shalt late ascend
And taste those Joys, which never will have End.
One Kiss -- farewel -- I can no longer stay,
My Guardian Angel summons me away: 220
Heaven guide thee and protect thee -- "

                    There her Breath
Stop'd, and she smiling sunk into the Arms of Death.
The Powers above, propitious to her Prayer,
Have made fair *O--n* their peculiar Care:
She doubly does her Sister's Charms possess,
And double Wisdom does the Beauty bless.

BUT oh! behold what Object, daz[z]ling bright,
Shines forth thus glorious to our wond'ring Sight,
As when fair *Luna* does in th' East appear,
And gilds with Silver Beams our Hemisphere,   230
No longer we observe the spangled Sky,
Or gaze upon the glimm'ring Gallaxy.
'Tis *M--s*, whose Beauty Love's great God disarms,
His Darts supplying with her surer Charms:
Crowds of Admirers court the conquering Fair,
But with Disdain she slights their anxious Care,
And scornfully rejects their humble Prayer.
Oh haughty Nymph ! like an eclipsing Cloud
Your Cruelty does all your Beauties shroud.
As when by Night black boisterous Storms arise,   240
Covering with dismal Darkness all the Skies,
Nor *Cynthia* shines, nor any twinkling Star,
To guide the poor benighted Traveller,
Wearied he wanders on in Paths unknown,

Wanting the Light of the beclouded Moon.
Thus *M--s* your Pride eclipses all your Light,
And wraps your sundry Charms in Shades of Night;
But if your Pity wou'd but sooth[e] their Smart,
Who for your Sake with Life it self wou'd part;
Nor wrack their throbbing Breasts with fatal Scorn,   250
(For you may Pity if not Love return)
Then shall your charms with chearing Lustre shine,
And the glad Swains in your just Praises join.

  BUT stop —— to loftier Strains I now aspire,
Ye Muses guide the Song, and *Phoebus* strike the Lyre;
Inspire my Soul with your extatick Flame,
The charming *O--ds* are my pleasing Theme.
The younger *O--d's* bright Celestial Face
Shines forth with every mild and blooming Grace;
Such lovely Blushes her fair Cheeks adorn,   260
As when at first appears the rosy Morn,
Whose radiant Blush a chearful Gladness yields,
Enliv'ning with its Rays the verdant Fields:
The verdant Fields at Morn's appraoch rejoice,
Whilst tuneful Choristers exalt their Voice,
When in their early Flight they wing their Way
To sing glad Anthems to the rising Day.
So, blooming Fair, your Beauties shine so bright,
The rest all vanish as the Shades of Night;
What pleas'd before can hardly now be seen,   270
Outshone by your superior Charms and Mien.

  BUT now, Behold the Sun of Beauty rise,
And dart his pointed Beams from Elder *O--d's* Eyes,
Who only, than her Sister, can display
More glorious Charms, and shine with brighter Ray:
Aurora she, but this is the Guide of Day.
As *Venus* rising from the liquid Plain,
Attended by the *Nereids* beauteous Train,
The beauteous Train in decent Order move,
Acknowledging the Sovereign Queen of Love: 280
Divinity so brightned in her Face,

On the strong Lustre none could dare to gaze;
Ev'n *Sol* himself confest his vast Surprize,
To see such Splendor from the Deeps arise,
And fear'd a Rival would contend for Sway,
And with him share the Government of Day.

WHEN great *Apelles*, emulous for Fame,
That Sea-born Goddess drew, each beauteous Dame
From ev'ry distant Part to th' Artist came,
That from their Charms he might conclude his Piece   290
The Wonder and Pride of ancient *Greece*;
Had then our *O--d* liv'd, from her alone
The Painter had the *Paphian* Goddess drawn;
Yet cou'd he ne'er have drawn the Piece aright,
So fair, so lovely, nor so wondrous bright:
Nature so well has finish'd ev'ry Part,
As far excels the Mimickry of Art;
Her brilliant Eyes, her graceful Charms and Mien,
Her Shape, her Air transcendently serene,
Proclaim the lovely Fair Beauty's unrival'd Queen.   300

OH ! that like *W--ll--r*, with such melting Lays
In tuneful Verse, I cou'd resound thy Praise,
The list'ning World should ring with *O--d*'s Name,
And *S--dn--y* yield to her more lasting Fame.
But 'tis in vain, my Muse can ne'er aspire
To *W--ll--r*'s Sweetness, or to *G--v--lle*'s Fire;
Yet still attempts, altho' with feeble Wing,
To stretch her infant Pinions forth and sing;
Whilst her first Flight she dedicates to thee,
To thee, Successour of victorious *G--*.   310
In thee thy Mother's conquering Beauties dwell,
And thine (if possible) ev'n hers excel;
From her, inherent Wisdom does abide
With thee, and Vertue over all preside.
But who shall tell thy vast, thy boundless Wit,
He who attempts to reach th' ætherial Height,
Like *Phaeton*, will perish in the Flight.
A Mind like thine alone can sing thy Worth,

An elevated Soul of Heav'nly Birth.
Henceforth *Orinda* shall no more be nam'd,   320
Nor soft *Astrea* longer shall be fam'd.

SEE, Female Wits, you must resign the Bays
To her whose Lyre sounds more melodious Lays:
In *O--d Sappho*'s Genius shines again,
Sappho, whose moving Lines gave ev'ry Bosom Pain.

BUT Oh ! the Godlike Beauties of her Soul,
Which gaudy Scenes of Vice cou'd ne'er controul.
What Muse can e'er reveal, or mount so high,
Her numerous, vast Perfections to descry!
Vertue in her has fixt her lasting Seat,   330
Vertue, which can alone make truly great.
Wit soon will perish; like a fading Flower,
Destructive Time will Beauty soon devour;
But o'er the Vertuous Mind Death has no Pow'r.
What Poets fancy, proves in *O--d* true,
Her Charms their Goddesses feign'd Charms subdue;
Juno's dread Majesty in her enshrin'd
With blooming *Hebe*'s sprightly Youth we find,
To the bright *Cyprian* Queen's soft Beauty join'd;
Diana's vertue her chast Bosom owns,   340
And the whole Maid *Minerva*'s Wisdom crowns.

OH ! Cou'd my Muse with an exalted Flight,
Of her Perfections reach the wondrous Height,
With Majesty sedate, with Beauty free,
Not starch'd, yet vertuous, wife, with Liberty;
Then wou'd I strive her glorious Name to raise
On lasting Pillars of enduring Praise.
But 'tis in vain, my Muse must down again,
Again retire to the more lowly Plain;
There must in doleful Lines my Grief express,   350
When Grief finds Vent in by Degrees grows less.

BUT Oh! my Sorrows never less can grow,
Still shall I sigh, and Tears will ever flow,

And still this fatal Pain my Soul must undergo.
Love's mighty Power has pierc'd my tender Breast,
His racking Tortures banish all my rest.
From *O--d*'s Eyes the forked Arrow came,
And kindled in my Soul an Hopeless Flame;
When her I view, my dreadful Pains encrease;
And Absence doubly does my Soul distress,   360
Nor dare I once presume to hope for Ease.
Unhappy as I am, my wayward Fate
Has plac'd me in too low, too mean a State;
My hapless Passion makes me pine away,
Weeping the Night I pass, and sighing spend the Day.
Yet I in Silence will resign my Breath,
No Trouble shall my saucy Flame bequeath
To the lov'd Fair, whom I will bless in Death.

AND oh! ye Powers! whate'er my Lot may prove,
On her show'r all your Blessings from Above: 370
Still may her Hours dance on with smiling Joy,
Free from corroding Grief's unkind Alloy.
That when her native Sky she shall ascend,
And ev'ry Doubt of Sorrow shall have End,   [of = or]
The Charmer, in that perfect State, may know
Blessings alone more great than those she left below.
                                          [alone = above]

FINIS

Josiah Martin's "Remarks"

Outside Cover:
Remarks on a Poem intituled The Fair Quakers [then MS addition:]
by Josiah Martin

First Page:
Remarks on a Poem, intituled The Fair Quakers. In a conference
between Hilary and Theophilus.
Non odi Poesin, neque Poetis male cupio: sed odi vitia Poeseos,
phrasesque idololatriam redolentes liberius perstringo, easque
radicitus evellere cupio. Pasor.
I am not an Enemy to Poetry, nor to Poets; but I hate the Vices of
Poetry, and the Phrases which savour of Idolatry, I pass a free
Censure upon, and should be glad they were totally banish'd.
LONDON: Printed by Ph. Gwillim in Austin-Fryers, and sold by J.
Morphew near Stationers Hall, 1714. Price 2d.

To the Reader.
Friendly Reader
    What Judgement soever thou may'st be inclin'd to pass upon
the following Conference, the Design of Publishing it is no other,
than to Promote Piety, and Discountenance that which appears
with a contrary Face, and manifestly tends to the Hurt of Christian
Discipline.
    A Person, who does not see how opposite the Poem (to which
this Conference relates) is to the Design of Christianity, must be

very little acquainted with the Holy Scriptures. And not only those Divine and Inspired Writings carry in them an Abhorrence to Things of the Nature of this Poem, but the Monuments of the Primitive Christians abundantly testifie against them. Sufficient Passages also might be produced from the works of Modern Authors, of no small Learning and Character, which do very much shew their dislike to such kind of Writing.

But if any should think the Poem too severely charged, let them look into Ecclesiastical History, where they will find Multitudes, both of Men and Women, undergoing most Cruel Tortures, for refusing to own, or call upon the Names of the Heathen Deities: And in Vindication of the Censure of this Poem, I shall give the Sense of a very Learned Author, to whom the Publick is not a little Indebted, for the Pains he has taken to assist Persons in Reading the Original Text of the New Testament: Speaking the best Method for Instructing Youth, he writes thus;

'Numbers of Christians, who liv'd under Heathen and Ungodly Emperors, upon saying, that the Names of the Heathen Gods were to be abominated, were presently Persecuted; and as may be seen in the *Acts of the Apostles*, in *Heb.* 11. 37. and *Ecclesiastical History*, were Whipp'd, Imprison'd, laid in Chains, Stoned, Sawn assunder, Burnt, Torn in Pieces by Wild Beasts. But our Pretenders to Poetry are not ashamed to Invoke the Muses, Pallas, &c. and laugh at us, who blame them for it, as over-scrupulous, and such as are afraid of our own shadows. But well may we say of them, O Preposterous and Unnatural Imitators! Such as Ape the Contemners and Enemies of the Author of our Religion! You might have liv'd very easily and peaceably in those Days among the Heathen; tho' they, at the same time, were the Death of the Apostles, and Multitudes of Martyrs, without any Mercy, because they would not Invoke Jupiter, Pallas, Phoebus, &c. But our Modern Poets, Retailers of Heathen Poetry, that have no more than the Name of Christians, attempt to excuse themselves, and tell us, they know all this well enough, and think otherwise, tho' they write thus: They know that Idols, and the Deities of the Heathen, are but Imaginary; and this is a Plea which the Corinthians used in defence of themselves. But as a just Answer to this, we may return what is in the following Passages of Holy Writ, I *Thess.* 5. 22. Abstain from all Appearance of Evil. 2. *Cor.* 7. 1. Let us cleanse our selves from all Filthiness of Flesh and Spirit, perfecting Holiness in the Fear of God. God would have us Worship him in Spirit, and with our Tongue, and to love him with all our Strength; and has created not only our Souls, but our Bodies, and would therefore have us Honour Him with both. *Rom.* 12. 1. Present your Bodies a living Sacrifice, holy, acceptable unto God. And truly I must openly call such Poets Heathens, and not Christians: For 'tis by their Language, I must judge, not being able to penetrate their Hearts. Therefore those who have spoke in a Heathenish Stile, I call Heathens.'

Remarks on a Poem, intituled The Fair Quakers, &c.

HILARY: How do'st do, Theophilus? Hast thou seen the New Poem on the Fair Quakers?

THEOPHILUS: Yes, Hilary, I have both seen and read it.

HIL: What is thy Opinion of it? Is it not a very Ingenious Poem?

THEO: I do not at all like it.

HIL: Pray what hast thou against it?

THEO: I think it is a very Licentious and Heathenish Poem.

HIL: That is Strange! I do not see any Liberty there, more than Poets sometimes take.

THEO: Yes, many more than are to be found in any Iuicious Christian Poet, which has fallen under my Reading.

HIL: But how dost thou make it out to be Heathenish, Theophilus?

THEO: Very easily; instead of imploring Divine Aid, the writer of this Poem calls upon the Nymphs and Pagan Gods to assist him, and compares his Fair Ones to their Goddesses; as if fit Examples were not to be found among Christians, or God's Chosen People under the Old Testament. Then again, his Stile, and Allusions to the Fictions of the Heathen Poets, make it rank Heathenism.

HIL: Thou art too severe, Theophilus, those are only Poetick Licences.

THEO: I know of no such Licences to be met with in the Christian Poets of Apostolick Times, nor in several Ages after; for the Primitive Christians, knowing how apt the Minds of Youth were to be taken with the Fictions and Fabulous Stories of the Heathen, labour'd to obliterate the Memory of them, by writing other pious and agreeable Poems, for Youth, in which the Holy Lives of the Patriarchs, Prophets, Saints and Martyrs, are very elegently set forth, and the History and wholesome Doctrine of the Old and New Testament were made their theme.

HIL: But allowance is to be made, according to the Subject; theirs being Divine, but this Juvenile and Gay.

THEO: What ever the Subject be, one who professeth Christianity, should write a Christian, and not a Heathenish Style.

HIL: The Author of this Poem is not alone; many Compositions of the like Nature and Stile, and rather worse, have been publish'd in our Age, by those who would not be esteem'd other than Christians.

THEO: The more is the pity; 'tis an Argument of great Degeneracy from the Spirit and Zeal of the Primitive Christians, who could not, I believe, have taken such Liberty, for the Whole World.

HIL: What then, must nothing of Poetry appear abroad, but what is written in a Divine Strain?

THEO: I do not say so; but I think a Christian Author is bound to make the Glory of God, or Good of his Neighbour, the end of his Writing.

HIL: If the end of Writing were only to raise an Innocent Cheerfulness, it might in some sense be said to contribute to a Person's Good; and I am inclin'd to think, the Author of this Poem meant no worse.

THEO: I have good Will to the Author, whoever he be, and so much Charity as to think, he meant only to Please and Divert by his Poem; But when I consider the Nature of the Thing, and the Manner it is wrote in, and that 'tis now made Publick, I am griev'd to consider the Evil Consequence of it.

HIL: Of what Evil Consequence can it be?

THEO: Have we not great Reason to fear the Ill Consequence of a Thing, which tends to the Ruine of Christian Virtues.

HIL: I do not see into that so clearly.

THEO: It may be thou hast not reflected so much on it as I have: But now I beseech thee to consider, is not the very Drift of the Poem to sooth and inflame a Natural Passion? Do not the Expressions and Comparisons tend to elevate the Mind, and to lead into Pride, which destroys the very Badge of a Christian, Humility.

HIL: But there are Lines in the Poem which extol, and give preference to a Virtuous Mind.

THEO: True, there are Three or Four Lines to that import; but what are those to the rest, which he bestows, and (as he says) *Dedicates to Beauty, Wit, a Fine Mein, &c.* Things no where taken notice of in the New Testament, as Graces of Women; who are exhorted to be adorn'd with Shamefacedness, and Good Works, and to be seen with the Ornaments of a Meek and Quiet Spirit, which is in the Sight of God of great Price?

HIL: May we not then, Theophilus, allow Beauty, Wit and Fine Shape, to be commendable Ornaments in Women?

THEO: Yes, as Natural Gifts, they are commendable in their Places; but we must not over-rate and prefer them to the Virtues of the Mind. But, Hilary, we are now beside the Arguments; I was not about to prove those Natural Gifts not commendable, purely as such; but that we cannot, as Christians, lawfully suffer our Minds to be taken up in the Contemplation of such Objects, in the Extravagant Manner of the Poem.

HIL: I know of no Law against it.

THEO: I am truly sorry for that, Hilary; I thought thou hadst been better acquainted with the Precepts of our Blessed Lord and Saviour Jesus Christ.

HIL: I remember Christ says, *Mat.* 5. 28. that whosoever looketh on a Woman to lust after her, hath committed Adultery already with her in his Heart; but I take that not to fall under the case we are now disputing.

THEO: My Intention is not to condemn the Author, but only to shew how Compositions of the Nature of his Poem run counter to the Spirit of the Gospel, or Mind of Christ, and therefore bring Dishonour upon our Holy Profession.

HIL: If I were convinced of that, I would say no more in its Vindication.

THEO: Well said, I intreat thee then, Hilary, to recollect: Thou hast read the Evangelists, can'st thou remember any Words of our Dear Lord and Saviour, which countenance the fomenting that Passion which the Poet (falsely) calls Love? Has he given Allowance to set up, and admire any thing in Man or Woman? Nay, does he not pronounce the Poor in Spirit, Blessed; those who Weep, and those who Hunger and Thirst after Righteousness? Does he not call for Self-denyal, and a taking up the Daily Cross? Does he not invite us, by his own Example, to Meekness and Lowliness in Heart? In fine, such as are persecuted and reviled for Righteousness, and his Name's Sake, such as love nothing in this World more than Jesus, are the Persons intituled to his Favour and Benedictions. Now Hilary, see what Agreement thou canst find between those Things, and the Language of this Poem.

HIL: I acknowledge, Theophilus, I find little Agreement; but I did not consider it in such a Light before.

THEO: I told thee, Hilary, thou hadst not reflected on it so much as I; for I must needs say, to me it not only appears Licentious and Irreligious, but to have an Immoral Tendency.

HIL: How Immoral, Theophilus? I can't perceive which way it can be said to tend to Immorality.

THEO: Let us first see if our Notions of what is Immoral agree. Immorality then, I take to be, That which in its own Nature tends to the Ruine of Civil Society; or, That which does or would hinder any Man from enjoying his Proper Right. Therefore whatsoever I do to another, which I would not he should do to me, (in the same Circumstances) is Unjust or Immoral.

HIL: Very good, thy Sentiments and mine, Theophilus, exactly agree; for I have thought, that Immorality is the very same as Injustice.

THEO: 'Tis so, Hilary, and without straining the Point over and above, upon Consideration, one shall quickly find, the Poem has an Immoral Tendency. For can any one say, the Design or Drift of the Poem is to give the Persons described a just or true Sight of Themselves? No, 'tis very plain, it Flatters them abominably. Now Flattery tends to blind the Eye, to puff up the Mind, and so leads to Pride (the most dangerous of Sins) and by consequence into Injustice, which is what we agreed to be Immoral.

HIL: Allowing it to lead into Pride, yet I do not so well perceive the Consequence.

THEO: No! is it not evident, that Proud Persons, who think better of themselves than they really are, (as from the Nature of Pride they must do;) I say, is it not evident, that at the same time those Persons think less, and meaner of others, than they really deserve? For by Nature we are all Equal. Where then do such Thoughts lead, but into Injustice?

HIL: But suppose that it goes no farther than Thought, where is the Injustice then?

THEO: We are told, *Mat.* 15. 19. that out of the Heart proceed evil Thoughts, Murders, Adulteries, Fornications, Thefts, False Witness, Blasphemies.

HIL: That is when Evil Thoughts are suffer'd to Lodge and Fix themselves in the Heart or Mind; but when 'tis only a Transient Thought, I can see no great Evil in that.

THEO: Right, an Evil Thought may come into a very Just and Holy Person's Mind; but meeting with no Reception, it cannot be charg'd on him as Evil: But Pride is so far from being only a Transient Evil Thought, that 'tis a Habit of Evil Thoughts.

HIL: Well, suppose it to be so.

THEO: Nay, 'tis undoubtedly so, Hilary, and from Pride I cou'd deduce the Injustice and Evils which have perplex'd Mankind ever since Adam.

HIL: O Wonderful!

THEO: Very true: Was it not Pride which cast Lucifer out of Heaven? Was it not Pride which the Serpent had inspir'd into our Mother Eve, that made her listen to his Voice; and thereby to transgress the Command of God. Now what follow'd, but Death, Calamity and Evils upon her whole Posterity?

HIL: Oh Frightful! O Amazing Consequences of Pride!

THEO: What must we now think of Persons, who value themselves on Performances, which not only lead into Pride, but Plunge the Minds of Youth into other very Gross Immoralities?

HIL: Truly, Theophilus, I think 'em little better than Heathens, notwithstanding they may go under the name of Christians.

THEO: Little better! I think 'em a great deal worse; for we may gather from the Lives and Morals of many of the Wise Heathens, that they made Virtue to consist in the Curbing and Restraint of Sensual Appetites: And some of them, acting by that Principle, did of Choice, live in so strict and self-denying a manner, as not only to abridge themselves of Superfluous Things, but hardly allow'd themselves the bare Necessities of Life.

HIL: They might then be said to have lived like True Christians.

THEO: Yes, Hilary, we may with good Reason call those Heathens Christians, and such loose Christians we are speaking of Heathens. And 'tis very much to be fear'd, such Heathens will rise up in Judgment against them.

HIL: 'Tis great Pity there shou'd be any such Christians.

THEO: 'Tis indeed, Hilary; but so long as Persons give way to an Ambitious Mind, and let loose the Reins of a Voluptuous Inclination, there is little Room to hope for Amendment.

HIL: I am well convinced of that, Theophilus: But I wonder what could make those Wise Heathens to choose so very Strict and Mortifying Ways of Living, since they could not be so well assur'd of Future Rewards and Punishments?

THEO: I cannot say how well they were assur'd, as to that; but from a Rational Inference they might conclude, that the Bountiful Author of their Nature, who was All-Wise and Just, would not suffer those, who (notwithstanding the Frowns and Opposition of the Wicked) endeavour'd to imitate his Divine Perfections, and to live up to the Law written in their Hearts: I say, they might very Rationally conclude, he would not suffer them to go Unrewarded, both here and hereafter. And as to their Way of Living, they saw that the Things of this World were Momentary and very Uncertain; and Experience told them, how insufficient they were to give their Minds solid Content. Then, by Reflecting on the Irregular Conduct of Men, and on the Evils which an Eager Pursuit of Riches and Grandeur, and the Indulgence of Sensuality brought into Civil Society, they judged it was much better to Copy after Nature, and to content themselves with Little.

HIL: Thy Reasons, Theophilus, seem to carry Weight with them; and thou mightest have added, that the Cares and Troubles of keeping Riches, when got, might have been a Motive to induce them to get clear of them.

THEO: Yes, Hilary, that might have been a very good Motive; and I have still another or two to advance, namely, First, a Superior Delight, which their Minds partook of, when least cumber'd with Worldly Things, and in a Contemplative State: And, Secondly, a Generous and Noble Desire to better Humane Society; this made them willing to be Exemplary, and to shew others what Methods were to be taken, to rectifie Disorders, and to preserve Tranquillity in Society.

HIL: And I believe they found the Delight and Satisfaction of Mind to increase proportionably, as they deny'd themselves of Sensual Enjoyments.

62

THEO: Our own Experience, Hilary, can best assure us of that. For my part, I have good Reason to believe, that all, who Devote themselves to a Contemplative Life, find, that Intellectual Pleasures do far transcend those of the Senses; and chiefly for this Reason, those Wise Heathens might make choice of a Self-denying Life, as being really the Happiest.

HIL: How much more Reason then have we, who profess Christianity, to choose the Self-denying Life, when the Reward of a Hundred-fold in this World, and Life Everlasting in the World to come, is promis'd by JESUS CHRIST to those who leave all for his Name's sake?

THEO: Well observ'd, Hilary, we have abundant more Reason to make choice of the Self-denying Life, as well from the Example of our Blessed Lord and Saviour, as from the Promises he has made us, in whose Mouth Guile was never found.

HIL: Oh, Theophilus! Methinks I now taste a Sweetness in those Words of our Lord, "Come unto me all ye that labour, and are heavy laden, and I will give you rest. Take my Yoke upon you, and learn of me, for I am Meek and Lowly in Heart, and you shall find rest to your Souls; for my Yoke is easie, and my Burthen is light", *Mat.* 11. 28, 29, 30.

THEO: I am glad, Hilary, to find those Words relish so well with thee: Oh how it were to be desired, that they did so with many more amongst us! They would not then take such Liberty as now they do.

HIL: O this Yoke! this Yoke! which can only ease the Soul, and bring it into its first Happy Frame.

THEO: The Lord increase those good Breathings in thy Soul, dear Hilary.

HIL: The Necessity of a Self-denying Life appears now to me with that Evidence and Force, that I cannot help being mov'd with Pity and Indignation: Pity, that so many among us, whose Parents have been to them as Good Monitors, and Bright Examples of a Holy Life; and they have refused to imitate them, because they would follow this World: And with Indignation at such, who would take it hard, not to be accounted Christians, and yet their Deportment and Conversation scandalize the very Heathens.

THEO: Charity begins at Home: Let us take the Apostle's Advice, *Phil.* 2. 12. and "work out our Salvation with Fear and Trembling": Let us give diligent heed to the Motions, and obey the Calls of the Holy Spirit in our Hearts; "for it is God who worketh in us both to will and to do of his good pleasure", as saith the same Apostle.

HIL: The Advice is wholesome and good; and 'tis much to be lamented, that Men of great Parts and Wit should so far slight it, as even to Ridicule the Expression of the Motions and Calls of the Spirit.

THEO: 'Tis no Wonder! For the Natural Man receiveth not the things of the Spirit of God, for they are foolishness unto him; neither can he know them, because they are spiritually discerned. The Voice of Wisdom is a still small Voice, not so easily heard in the Hurry of Passions. When God speaks to Man, 'tis generally in the Cool of the Day, when his Passions are quiet, and his lofty Imaginations and Thoughts are brought down.

HIL: Happy will it be for him, who hearkens to the Reproofs of Wisdom, and loves the Hand that corrects him. For by Afflictions we are made Wise, as may be inferr'd from the Words of David, "Before I was afflicted, I went astray".

THEO: Thy Observation, Hilary, is very true. The way to Wisdom, is a State of Humility: For 'tis said, God teaches the Humble, and guides the Meek in Judgement. We may now wind up the Argument, having made it appear, that Mankind derive their Happiness from Humility, and their Evils from Pride; and that Wisdom is to be obtain'd by no other way, than that of Self-denial, and taking up the Daily Cross; I mean, that Wisdom which cometh from above, which is first Pure, then Peaceable, Gentle, and easie to be Intreated, full of Mercy and good Works, without Partiality, and without Hypocrisie.

HIL: I am now, dear Theophilus, fully confirm'd, that to be made truly Wise and Happy, is to obey the Commands of Christ, who was himself a perfect Pattern of Humility and Self-denial.

THEO: 'Tis certainly so, let Men pretend to what they will; there is no other Way, but Christ the Power and Wisdom of God: They therefore, who attempt to climb up another Way, will be found Thieves and Robbers.

HIL: O the Beauty! O the loveliness of a Humble Soul! How am I delighted with the Idea which is now presented to my Mind? Methinks I see Drusilla, at her Publick Devotion, strowing the Floor with her Tears, like Mary at the Feet of Jesus.

THEO: A very Lovely Sight indeed, Hilary! Our Dear Lord himself was highly pleas'd in beholding the same; and by many Places in Holy Writ, we find, that the Contrite in Spirit, and the Broken-Hearted, are in a peculiar manner God's Favourites.

HIL: Oh that we had more such Humble and Contrite Souls among us! How would they Honour their Profession? Triphosa, Meek and Patient Triphosa, comes in my view: O how lovely, how Taking is her Deportment! How Condescending to her Parents! How loving, Sweet and Engaging to her Brothers and Sisters, and to all her Friends! When I have beheld her in Company, I have said in my Heart, what so Beautiful, what so Attracting as the Soul tinctured with Truth!

THEO: Nothing, Hilary, there is nothing in this World so Lovely, and so Attracting. Truth draws Esteem and Veneration from its very Enemies: The most Wicked Person sometimes will commend the Pious and Just; which verifies the Promise of God, who hath said, He that Honours me, him I will Honour.

HIL: I see, Theophilus, yea, now I see the Heavenly Effects of following Jesus in the Way of Self-denial; Oh that I had my self given more heed to his Calls and Wooings in my Heart!

THEO: Did we all listen to his Voice, who stands at the Door and Knocks, and did we obey his Calls, then would the Knowledge of the Lord fill the Earth, as Waters cover the Sea. There would be no hurt, no destroying. Nation would not lift up Sword against Nation, nor learn War any more. The Wolf would dwell with the Lamb. And then would the Earth enjoy her Sabbath.

HIL: Oh, Theophilus, my Heart is touch'd, sensibly touch'd, with the Libertines amongst us, whose Ways frustrate those Blessed Effects of the Gospel.

THEO: Let us pray to the Lord for them; it may be he will reach to their Hearts in time, and let them see the Loveliness of Truth, beyond the Ways they now delight in.

FINIS.

A FUNERAL ELEGY
On the Death of John Bingley

No longer Muse, no longer take thy Flights,
In pleasing Strains of Love and soft Delights;
But from thy Temples rend the *Myrtle* Boughs
And Baleful *Cypress* twine about thy Brows.
Thus Mourn the Dear Departed CELADON,
PARNASSUS' Bride, and PHOEBUS' Darling Son.

THOU who dost at the Funeral Rites appear
In Sable Weeds attir'd, and flowing Hair,
Most mournful of the Nine; conduct along
The Trembling Lyre, and aid the Falt'ring Song.   10

YE Lovely Virgins, whose deserved Worth
He whilome sweetly sung, and warbled forth;
Come pay your grateful Tribute at his Urn!
And share my Griefs; with me Lament and Mourn!
Lament the Youth, now clos'd in Death's cold Arms,
Who'll sing no more your *Beauties,* or your *Charms!*
Come, Gentle Swains! with Tear-distilling Eyes
Approach, and with my Sorrows sympathize:
Let nothing on the Flowr'y Plain be heard,
But loud Laments for the Melodious BARD,   20

Whose pleasing *Conversation* will no more
Your tedious Hours beguile, as heretofore.
Come, Tender Lovers! who have left the Smart,
And cruel Torments of a *bleeding Heart*!
Who have been fetter'd in a Tyrant's Chain,
And tortur'd by a scornful Nymphs Disdain,
Show your compassion for the Faithful SWAIN.
Let flowing Tears, like boundless *Nile*, arise!
And weep a briny Deluge from your Eyes!

SWEET was his *Carriage*, unreserv'd his *Mind*:   30
His *Temper* Pleasing, Gentle, Free and Kind.
His Courteous *Nature* shew'd no Spark of Pride,
Or Self-Conceit, did with his Wit reside.
In soft Tranquillity he led his Life,
From *Sorrow* free, and from corroding Grief:
Each circling Hour in Blissful Ease was spent;
And ev'ry Day encreas'd his sweet *Content*;
(Thrice happy SWAIN!) till an envenom'd Dart,
From O—d's Eyes, inflam'd his Gentle Heart:
Inflam'd his *Heart*, and pierc'd his Tender *Breast*,
That he nor Night nor Day enjoy'd his *Rest*!   40
For her he sigh'd, (Dear BARD!) for her he Mourn'd,
And all his former *Joys* at once to *Sorrow* turn'd!

LONG did the Bleeding Youth his Flame conceal,
Afraid his hopeless Passion to reveal.
Long, with his utmost Pow'r and Art, he strove
To stop the mighty Torrent of his Love,
And live unsacrific'd to her Disdain:
But ah! his best Endeavours prov'd in vain,
His Love encreas'd, and still encrease'd his Pain.
Since therefore Silence did his Woes augment,   50
At last, in Melting Lays, he gave his Passion vent.

BUT, O ye Pow'rs! with what Ætherial Fire
And Godlike Skill he struck th' Entrancing Lyre!
How soft his Strains! with what inviting Air!
And with what moving Grace he sung the Fair!
Serenely his Immortal Numbers shine:
And beauteous Thoughts adorn his ev'ry Line.
If he in gentle Raptures deigns to sing,
Or soar aloft with more expanded Wing;
His flowing Wit, and streaming Eloquence,

Do still attract our Souls, and ravish ev'ry Sense.   60
No word throughout his Theme can find a Place
To stain, with rosy Dye, the purest Face:
But from all nauseous Pedantry refin'd,
With polish'd *Art*, and native *Sweetness* join'd:
His inoffensive Muse each *Sex* inspires
With vestal Flames, and chast Hymenial Fires.

HERE did the wounded SWAIN disclose his Grief,
And so pathetically sought relief,
That 'twou'd have mollified a Heart of Flint,
Or made the most obdurate Breast relent,   70
Had not his ardent Flame to One been bold,
Whose Favour only cou'd be gain'd with Gold,
Accursed Gold! to whose Imperial Sway,
Our Modern NYMPHS such Adorations pay,
That neither Virtue now, nor Wit can move
Their stupid Minds, with, its Aid, to Love!
'Twas this that caus'd the Cruel Maid to hear
His Suit with Scorn, and slight his humblest Pray'r.

THE YOUTH astonish'd stood at such Disdain,
And thence despairing ever to obtain   80
A Glimpse of Favour, banish'd from her Sight,
In Bliss and Pleasure took no more Delight:
Each setting Sun left him o'erwhelmed with Grief,
Nor the returning Light could yield Relief.
But more and more his poinant Pain encreas'd,
The swelling Anguish of his throbbing Breast;
Till scorning Limits longer shou'd controul
Its way, it forc'd a Passage thro' his Soul!
Depriv'd the Lovely Youth of Vital Breath,
And threw him in the cold Embrace of Death!   90
Whose Spirit, thus freed from its Earthly Chain,
Ascending, mounted to th' Empyreal Plain:
Where, in Seraphic Lays, he sweetly sings
Eternal Anthems to the King of Kings.

THUS Blooming CELADON was snatch'd away,
When Nature look'd so Flourishing and Gay:
Thus He! the Pride and Glory of his Age,
For *Wit* and *Humour*! vanish'd off the Stage!
Like some fair Flower, that beatifies the Field,
Which does to blasting Mildews Fading yield.   100

Tho' undistinguished from the Vulgar Train,
Interr'd in Dust his Body does remain:
Tho' no ambitious *Pyramid* rehearse
His Memory; yet his *Immortal* Verse
Shall raise a Monument, that will surpass
Or *Parian* Marble, or *Corinthian* Brass:
Which (when the Piles, that once in Lustre blaz'd,
Are by th'inveterate Teeth of Time defac'd,
Fixt on the Pillars of enduring Fame,
Shall to Eternity preserve his NAME.   110

FINIS